CROSSING THE
BLUE MOUNTAINS

CROSSING THE BLUE MOUNTAINS

Journeys through two centuries,
from naturalist Charles Darwin
to novelist David Foster

First published in 1997 by Duffy & Snellgrove
PO Box 177 Potts Point NSW 2011 Australia
dands@magna.com.au

Distributed by Tower Books (02) 9975 5566

Cover by Alexandra Snellgrove
Typeset by Maggie Cooper in Bembo

Printed by Australian Print Group

Cover: Postcard (details unknown) held by the Mitchell Library,
Sydney, which also holds William Romaine Govett's *Accident on
the Road at Victoria Pass*, reproduced after page 38 in this book.

All photographs in the book are reproduced with the permission
of the photographer, Ian Brown.

ISBN 1 875989 11 0

CONTENTS

LIST OF MAPS

LIST OF ILLUSTRATIONS

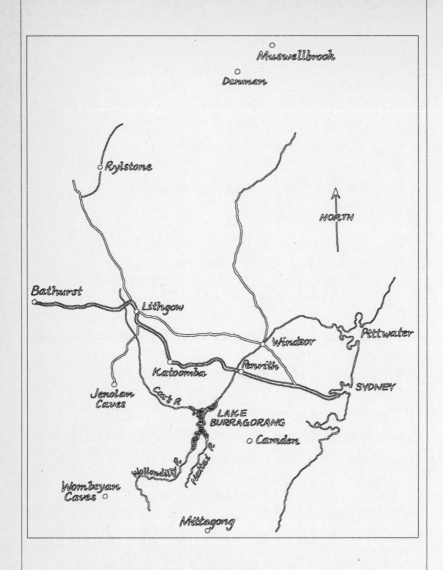

Map 1: The Blue Mountains are now considered to
extend from just below Denman in the north almost to
Mittagong in the south. Much of this area consists of national
parks (Wollemi, Blue Mountains, Kanangra-Boyd, Nattai).
Cox's River runs east through the mountains into Lake
Burragorang (Warragamba Dam), the Nepean and
then the Hawkesbury rivers.

Publisher's Introduction

This book contains eleven personal accounts of crossing the Blue Mountains. Ten of them come from the period between the first white settlement in 1788 and the gold rushes of the 1850s, a time when the crossing was arduous, exciting, and novel. Many people left accounts of their journeys; those in this book have been chosen for their literary and entertainment qualities.

Here you will find Barrallier, the French royalist who used Aborigines as his guides, fascinated by their customs and horrified at the way the men treated the women. Here is Elizabeth Hawkins in 1822, shepherding her eight children, aged from one to twelve, and her seventy-year-old mother across the mountains along a dirt track, soon after arriving from England. In the midst of her struggles, one dusk, she suddenly finds herself feeling strangely happy. 'It was a moment I shall never forget. For the first time for many a long month I seemed capable of enjoying and feeling the present moment without a dread for the future. 'Tis true we had in a manner bade adieu to the world, to our country and our friends, but in our country we could no longer provide for our children, and the world from that cause had lost all its charm.'

Here too is Major Anthill, the war hero with Governor and Mrs. Macquarie's party, whose main concern in the mountains seems to have been to get a good night's sleep, and Justice Barron Field, the amateur poet, scanning the gum trees as he trots along, desperate for a familiar metaphor. Here is Charles Darwin, finding an important insight on the bank of the Cox's River that was to contribute to the theory of evolution.

Taken together these stories make up what I hope is a good book of Australian travel writing. They are distinguished from more modern books by their depth of curiosity and absence of meanness. Among their authors you will find no equivalent of Paul Thoreaux or Bill Bryson, who seem to travel the world in search of things to complain about and people to laugh at. The writers in this book come not to sneer but to live. Their accounts are written by adults, with a thirst for new experience and a curiosity and enthusiasm regarding what it was that Britain was building here in the first half of the nineteenth century.

Such positive attitudes might strike the modern reader as strange. The most widely read work of Australian history in the past decade is probably Robert Hughes' *The Fatal Shore*. Many people have come away from it with the general impression that Sydney in its first decades was a combination of torture chamber and charnel house. This was not Hughes' intention, which was rather to remind readers of elements of the convict experience which he believed had been written out of our history. But his book was so well written, and so widely read, that it affected the way many people regard early Australian history. *Crossing the Blue Mountains* provides a very different picture, and it is worth pointing out that there is scholarly support for a more upbeat view of early white Australian history. Historian Alan Frost has written a book, *Botany Bay Mirages*, refuting some of the 'black armband' myths regarding Sydney's early days. One of Frost's points is that the smallpox which had such a terrible effect on the Aborigines around Port Jackson in 1789 almost certainly came not from the First Fleet but from Macassan (Indonesian) fishermen working on the north coast of Australia, from where it spread south. The part of Frost's argument most relevant to this book is that, following the difficult first four years, Sydney was one of the most successful European colonies anywhere in the world. Western civilization bloomed here more quickly and more fully than perhaps anywhere else. This was noted by many early travellers, including a number of French observers. It was demonstrated by the reluctance of so many of the settlers, whether they had come here free or in chains, to return to Europe. The convicts themselves worked shorter hours than agricultural labourers in England. When they gained their freedom, they had no trouble getting jobs which paid several times the English wages, and which could, in time, have paid for their voyage back to England, had they wished to go. Most did not. (As Robert Hughes wrote: 'assignment worked'.) Many of them became successful farmers and, in some cases, businessmen. This is the exciting and prosperous world described by the writers in this book, men and women who had crossed the seas, in Frost's words, 'expecting to find a periphery of the European world [but who] instead found a centre.'

The words 'Australia' and 'Australians' were already in use to describe this centre. The first newspaper called the *Australian*, no relation to the present one, was founded by Blue Mountains explorer William Charles Wentworth in 1824. In 1836 Charles Darwin was told by some young women at the Macarthurs' house: 'Oh, we are Australians and know nothing of England.'

Among the reasons Frost gives for the colony's success was the unique depth and extent of English interest in horticulture. Many early visitors noted the flourishing gardens around cottages in Sydney and Parramatta, and this was just one manifestation of a popular enthusiam, backed by the knowledge acquired in the scientific revolution in Britain in the eighteenth century, which also demonstrated itself in the increasingly successful farms on the Cumberland Plain. The modern reader cannot but notice how interested most of the writers in this book were—no matter how far removed from agriculture their occupations—in details of farming, just as some of them show a considerable interest in, and knowledge of, natural science in general. Most people in the late twentieth century who can write as well as the authors in this book would, if they took a similar journey today, be blind to many of the things observed with such interest by these men and women of 150 years ago.

One exception is Australian novelist David Foster, whose observational skills were perhaps developed by his training and work as a scientist. Foster's first novel, *The Pure Land*, is set partly in Katoomba, and his most recent, *The Glade within the Grove*, takes place largely in a valley in another part of the Great Dividing Range. For this book he walked through the bush from near Mittagong to Katoomba, his birthplace, and reflected on being alone in the bush, on what Wilderness means to us today, and on the difficulty a white person can still have in relating to the eucalyptus.

As Foster's essay shows, the European encounter with the Blue Mountains has involved not just a physical journeying but an imaginative one. It has also involved the intellectual and the scientific, and this is acknowledged in this book by a description of the discovery of the Wollemi Pine by Doug Noble, and the excitement and horticultural experiments that followed.

A major reason the Cumberland Plain could be turned into a version of England so soon after 1788 was because much of it was already clear, thanks to Aboriginal fire farming. Encounters with Aborigines, and reports of their customs, from the use of fire to cannibalism, form one of the most interesting parts of the following stories. European attitudes range from fear through curiosity to pity. The Aborigines themselves, too, had a range of attitudes. For some of them, the arrival of the Europeans, whatever else it was, was a great intellectual adventure. We see them, throughout the book, approaching and withdrawing. We also, tragically, see them dying, their numbers dwindling.

When this book was almost completed I searched it for a title, seeking among the nineteenth century accounts for a romantic phrase, something redolent of a sense of grandeur or triumph, of the conquest of the west. There was nothing. What impressed me often was the colloquial character of much of the writing, its direct humour, confidence and lack of adornment or airs. Historian Russel Ward would have us believe the Australian character derives from a background of suffering, of rural workers, battlers and unions. But the tone in the writing of most of these English men and women of 150 years ago resembles something to be found in many Australians I know today. Perhaps it was the tone of the Georgian middle class, or that section of it which chose to come to this country, modified by what it found here. It lacks aristocratic qualities and is confident, educated, curious, and imbued by the middle-class virtues. Maybe there is more of this in Australians than it has been fashionable to admit in the past decades.

Many people think of the Blue Mountains as the landscape around Katoomba. In point of geographic fact, the land perimeter of the Cumberland Plain around Sydney consists of a string of sandstone plateaux running from north of the Hunter Valley down through Wollemi National Park and Kanangra-Boyd to Mittagong. An important feature of these is the Cliff Wall, an often broken, generally west-facing line of cliffs, of varying heights, which runs from the Broken Back Range of the Hunter Valley south for about 280 kilometres. Its most famous points are the edge of the King's Tableland just south of Wentworth Falls (highest point about three hundred metres) and Narrow Neck at Katoomba. The term 'the Blue Mountains' is increasingly applied to much of this area by scientists, rangers and bushwalkers, and this is the way the term is understood in this book.

    The area around Katoomba, despite popular misconception, is not part of the Great Dividing Range. This lies much further west, just beyond Lithgow. The Divide is so-called because it is the line between those rivers running west and those which run east. The Cox's River, even though it has its source beyond Lithgow, actually runs through the mountains, becoming the Warragamba Dam and then the Nepean and Hawkesbury rivers before reaching the sea at Pittwater. Thus some of the people in this book, while they crossed the Blue Mountains, did not cross the Great Divide.

Many people tried to cross the mountains before Barrallier, whose 1802 journeys open the book. In 1789 Governor Philip led a party in boats up the Nepean River as far as the Grose River, where the water became too shallow for them to continue. Members of the party walked up Richmond Hill and became the first Europeans to enter the Blue Mountains, then known as the Carmarthen Hills. In the next ten years more tentative explorations were undertaken by Watkin Tench, William Dawes, George Bass and others. The most successful seems to have been John Wilson, a former convict who possibly went as far west in the 1790s as Blaxland's party was to do—with considerably more acclaim—in 1813. But before Blaxland's journey there was not much motivation for crossing the mountains. Indeed, it seems to have suited the governors to have an impenetrable mountain range around Sydney to stop the convicts escaping. The most successful official expedition before 1813 was in 1797, when Governor Hunter asked Wilson to take some convicts on an expedition to prove to them that China, contrary to a myth widely believed among the Irish, did not lie just across the mountains.

Most of the historical accounts that follow come from a wonderful scholarly book edited by George Mackaness called *Fourteen Journeys Over the Blue Mountains of New South Wales 1813-1841*, last published in 1965. They have been heavily edited for the present volume to make them accessible to the general reader. I am most grateful to Mackaness for introducing me to these accounts and for his notes on them. For more information see the Sources section at the end of this book. Readers of traditional disposition should be reassured that the frequent use of 'z' instead of 's' (as in 'civilization') follows the English spelling of the early nineteenth century rather than the American usage of the late twentieth.

The photographs in the book are by Ian Brown, a district operations manager with the N.S.W. National Parks and Wildlife Service based at Blackheath who has been bushwalking and photographing in the mountains for twenty-five years. His work, as well as possessing great pictorial qualities, expresses an intimacy with, and knowledge of, the subject which is quite rare. We're very fortunate that he's allowed some of his work to be reproduced here.

Michael Duffy

I

Francis Barrallier

An embassy to the King of the Mountains

I n 1802 Governor King sent Francis Barrallier, an ensign
in the New South Wales Corps, to try to find a way across
the Blue Mountains towards the south-west. He wanted
Barrallier to investigate the belief, held by some convicts and
apparently based on stories told by Aborigines, that there was
a white settlement just over the mountains. For some reason
which we do not know, Barrallier was not given a copy of
the record of John Wilson's expeditions five years before.
He was due to start in May but rain delayed him until much
later in the year. He made several journeys from his depot
near the Nattai River, about twenty kilometres north-west
of Picton, and seems to have travelled over fifty kilometres
west, although, his journal entries being somewhat confusing, there are at least eight different published guesses about
his route. The most recent, by historian Chris Cunningham,
has Barrallier turning back at the falls on Burnt Hole Creek,
south-west of Kanangra Walls.

In the end Barrallier had no luck in getting through the
Nattai-Wollondilly river system. He was, however, a capable
explorer and made good use of local Aborigines as guides. He
was also a curious observer and a capable writer, and left a

journal which contains some fascinating accounts of the Aborigines and their customs. The Aborigines' tomahawks, to which he refers, had been obtained from Europeans.

The wild cattle described in Barrallier's account were those which had escaped from the government herd following settlement in 1788. These had strayed to the area around Camden which became known as the Cowpastures, where John Macarthur received a large grant of land in 1804.

The extracts from Barrallier's journal are preceded by a letter from Governor King to Joseph Banks. The Colonel Paterson refered to was commander of the New South Wales Corps, an organisation that was the spiritual predecessor of today's New South Wales Police Service.

I have informed you in my several letters of the great use Ensign Barrallier, of the New South Wales Corps, was of to me and the public … in making a partial journey to the mountains, which was introductory to his undertaking the journey he afterwards performed, but which I was obliged to effect by ruse, as Col. Paterson had very illiberally informed me that officers being at all detached from their regimental duty was contrary to the instructions he had from the Duke of York. In consequence, I was obliged to give up his services after this unhandsome claim, but claimed him as my aide-de-camp, and that the object of discovery should not be totally relinquished, I sent him on an embassy to the King of the Mountains.

He was gone six weeks and penetrated 137 miles among them beyond the Nepean. His journal being written in such an unintelligible hand, I have not been able to get it translated or copied …

Extract from a private letter to Sir Joseph Banks from Philip Gidley King, Governor of New South Wales, 9 May 1803.

From Parramatta I went to Prospect Hill with my party, composed of four soldiers, belonging to the New South Wales Corps, and five convicts. I found at that rendezvous one of the natives of the Cow Pastures, named Gogy, whom I had engaged to accompany me ... When passing Carabeely, we saw a kangaroo which we killed, and after half-an-hour's walk we entered a valley where there was a herd of wild cattle. I counted 162 of them peaceably pasturing; they only perceived my party when it was at a short distance from them. The cattle advanced several times, as if they were going to attack us, and I had the greatest difficulty in making them leave the place and allow my party to pass. I had even to send my men to pursue them, uttering loud shouts ...

In the swamps of Manhangle, Carabeely, and others, enormous eels, fishes and various species of shells are found, which are sometimes used by the natives as food. They usually feed upon opossums and squirrels, which are abundant in that country, and also upon kangaroo-rat and kangaroo, but they can only catch this last one with the greatest trouble, and they are obliged to unite in great numbers to hunt it. When the natives assemble together to hunt the kangaroo, they form a circle which contains an area of one or two miles, according to the number of natives assembled. They usually stand about thirty paces apart, armed with spears and tomahawks. When the circle is formed, each one of them holding a handful of lighted bark, they at a given signal set fire to the grass and bush in front of them. In proportion as the fire progresses they advance forward with their spears in readiness, narrowing the circle and making as much noise as possible, with deafening shouts, until, through the fire closing in more and more, they are so close as to touch one another. The kangaroos, which are thus shut into that circle, burn their feet in jumping on every side to get away, and are compelled to retire within the circle until the fire attacks them. They then try to escape in various directions, and the natives frightening them with their shouts throw their spears at the one passing nearest to them. By this means not one can escape. They roast the product of their chase, without skinning nor even gutting the animals, and then divide it among themselves, after having cut each animal into pieces …

At eleven in the morning I found myself near a ditch filled with water. I halted there, and gave orders to skin the kangaroo which was prepared for our dinner. The heat being excessive, I allowed my men to rest until four o'clock.

After having walked for a little while, I perceived two natives seated under a bush, one of whom seemed as if he were anxious to run away, while the other one remained seated, and appeared to be trying to persuade the former to stay. Gogy, the native I had in my service, started running, and went and sat with them, where he remained until we arrived. He came and told me that one of these natives was a mountaineer called Bungin, and the other knew the white men, and was called Wooglemai. Wooglemai, in the natives' language, signifies 'one-eyed'. This native knew Gogy, as he used to go from time to time to Parramatta and Prospect Hill. The mountaineer called Bungin was an inhabitant of the south, and had left the Canambaigle tribe because they wanted to kill him. He was the brother of a famous chief who had accidentally killed himself in falling from a tree. That chief was called Goonboole. He inhabited the mountains near Jervis Bay, and was the terror of the neighbourhood.

I went to the mountaineer to examine a mantle with which he was covered. This mantle was made of skins of various animals sewed together. It was a very great curiosity, and as I was desirous of obtaining it, I proposed to him to exchange it for a new axe, but he would not part with it, and told me that the nights were very cold and his mantle was his only covering. I was compelled to abandon my proposal, and in order to attach to me this mountaineer, who would be very useful to me in the country I was in, I had the head of the kangaroo given to him to appease his hunger, after which he came and proposed, as a token of friendship, to exchange his old axe for the new one I had offered him for his mantle. I filled him with joy by complying with his request.

I resumed my journey at half past five o'clock, and arrived with my party and baggage on the border of a small creek, where I decided to stay for the night. Nearly the whole of the country from Binheny to Carabeely being open towards the south, presents perspectives of surprising beauty. The hills in the same direction, rising insensibly the one above the other, confounding themselves with the first ranges of mountains, offer to the sight a variety of scenes of the most picturesque aspect. But I have seen only a few spots where the soil could be adapted for cultivation, and they were liable to be inundated by the overflowing of the rivers. The place where I decided to spend the night was on the territory of the mountaineer Bungin. He gave a proof of his friendship and gratefulness for my good treatment by building a hut for me, and I was very thankful for his kind attention. The natives do not allow any stranger to inhabit the territories they have appropriated to themselves. They themselves build huts for the strangers they wish to receive as friends. I was then at about two miles from a chain of mountains, the direction of which is westerly, inclining towards the south; southerly there is a range of hills stretching in various directions ...

On the 8th November I crossed the creek, the banks of which are nearly perpendicular; but the bullocks succeeded in making a wide passage, quite practicable for men on foot, but too steep for a carriage to pass, and I was obliged to have the wagon carried by hand to the other side. I walked until noon, when I stopped near another creek in order to rest ourselves until four o'clock. A soup made of boiled rice, with pickled pork, composed our repast, and I saw that the two natives had their share; but whilst one of the newly arrived mountaineers would not partake of this food, the other ate it with avidity. The former having caught a lizard, roasted it, and devoured it. I tasted some of it, and preferred it to the opossum.

Besides lizards and other animals, grubs are eaten by the natives, and it is more particularly those which are found in the trunks of trees they look for. For this purpose they always carry with them a switch about twelve inches long and of the thickness of a fowl's feather, which they stick into their hair above the ear. One of the extremities of this stick is provided with a hook. When they discover on the trunk of a tree the mark of the hole made by some of these grubs, they make the hole larger with their axe, and if they are certain that the grub is there they dip their switch into the hole, and, by means of the hook, draw it out, and eat it greedily. It is a delicacy of which they never get tired.

The ground travelled over during the morning consisted of heights quite easy of access from the creek, whence I had started. I noticed that the trees are generally what is called blue-gum, ironbark, stringybark and yellow-gum. The soil is mostly bad, and after having passed the heights at a distance of about two miles from the larger creek, a vast plain is found, which is full of kangaroos. The soil there is formed of white clay, covered with iron ore, and is extremely bad.

I resumed my journey at four, and at six o'clock crossed another creek. After having travelled over a plain, I perceived fires in several places, and Bungin told me that it was a chief called Canambaigle with his tribe, who were hunting, and had on that very day set the country on fire. He showed me the imprints of various feet, both of males and females, scattered here and there …

On the 9th November, at six in the morning, when I was preparing to start, Bungin … told me that he heard the voice of a native at some distance from us, and, after having spoken to Gogy, they went together towards the spot whence the sound of the voice had appeared to come. I heard them repeat, several times, the word coo-ee, shouting with all their strength; and a quarter of an hour after I had lost sight of them they came back, bringing two other mountaineers with them. One was called Bulgin and the other Wallarra. The latter had never seen a white man, but the former had seen several whilst kangaroo hunting. Wallarra was seized with a great fright when I stepped forward to shake hands with him, and I was obliged to withdraw and leave him with the other natives, who tried to reassure him and give him confidence, telling him that I did not do them any harm, that I had come to gather some pebbles and plants, and that I had the animals skinned to preserve their fur.

I had some boiled rice and sugar given to them. Bulgin ate it with greediness, but Wallarra ate only the sugar, which I had to put on top. It would be difficult to describe his fright. He was standing with crossed arms and his eyes riveted on the ground. I had a second handful of sugar given to him, which he ate; but when I again went near him, his whole frame began to tremble.

The forenoon was already far advanced. I gave orders to yoke the bullocks to the wagon … The sight of the bullocks being yoked to the wagon was a new cause of fright to the new mountaineer, and the other natives had a great deal of trouble in making him come back. When the wagon was put in motion they followed all its movements, making all sorts of grimaces, and speaking with a great velocity expressive of their astonishment. I understood that they were beginning to tame him, because Bulgin came to tell me they were going to fetch their wives and two little children they had left in the forest, and that they would come to join me at Nattai as soon as they had found them.

After dinner I took two men with me and went down the creek, which I followed until dusk, gathering flowers and fragments of a rather peculiar sandstone. I returned to the depot at sunset, and about the same time Bulgin … with Bungin, arrived with their wives and two children; but Wallarra, the other mountaineer, was not with them. The newly arrived natives lighted a fire on the left-hand side of the depot. Gogy associated with them, but his wife, who, with her child, was at some distance from that spot, did not leave the place where she was. From there she watched with great interest what was taking place between the natives and her husband on the side opposite. The natives of this country are inclined towards superstition and believe in the existence of an evil spirit.

Gogy told me that they had brought portions of a

monkey (in the native language 'colo') [koala] but they had cut it in pieces, and the head, which I should have liked to secure, had disappeared. I could only get two feet through an exchange which Gogy made for two spears and one tomahawk. I sent these two feet to the Governor in a bottle of spirits.

Gogy had built for me a very large hut, made with the bark of the trees, and had erected it just opposite the hut of my people. I had some fire lighted in it and carried my effects there. After having regulated the night service and placed the sentry at his post, I prepared to spend the night in my hut. My men and the natives retired to their respective quarters ...

Generally speaking, the plants there are of the same kind as those growing near Sydney. The foot of the mountains is within a gunshot of either side of the river, and, as far as I could judge, they are more than half a mile in height, and one could only reach the summit of a very small number of them. These mountains are generally accessible up to a certain height, but at an altitude of a quarter of a mile they are perpendicular, and their summit forms a kind of leaden wall. More generally they overhang in the form of vaults, in the interior of which one sees enormous rocks overhanging, and quite ready to fall down at the slightest move, thus taking away from anyone's mind the idea of seeking there for a shelter against the rain, for fear of being crushed down by their downfall ...

At about 4 pm, I perceived on a hill three kangaroos, which did not appear to be frightened; but they fled when I sent one of my men to shoot them. I noticed that the red coats of my soldiers put the kangaroos to flight as soon as they perceived them, and we could only shoot one when I had made them take off their coats.

At 6 pm, I arrived in a valley, where I found two ponds. Bulgin, the mountaineer, told me that he had stopped several days in this place, and that he had caught very large eels in the ponds. Gogy having discovered a parrot's nest in the trunk of a blue-gum, cut steps in the tree with his axe;

but when he reached the nest he found only some eggs, which he offered to me. My refusal of them he regarded as an insult.

This spot seemed to me convenient to rest at during the night. I made Gogy cut a hut for me, and I had it placed on the slope of a hill, whence I could enjoy a view of the ponds and of the noble aspect of the mountains surrounding me on the east and west.

Half an hour before dusk I heard a noise which I mistook for the lowing of several oxen, but I was undeceived in learning it was the croak of frogs of a tremendous size which were in the pond ...

The mountains on the left side of the river trend south-westwardly, and the width of the plain, from the foot of the mountains on the opposite range, is two and a half miles. This plain widens in proportion as one advances south-west-wardly, the two ranges inclining the one towards the south, the other towards the west. The bed of this new river [the Wollondilly] is considerably wider than that of the Hawkesbury River. During the summer it is partly dry; but it has the disadvantage of not being navigable on account of a number of waterfalls [rapids], which completely bar its bed. It appears that, in the winter, the waters rise ten or twelve feet above the waterfalls, and carry away pieces of granite of various colours and other stones. The water is teeming with different species of fishes and shells, which are of the same kind as those in the first river.

At one o'clock in the afternoon, I halted for dinner, and I caused the grass to be burnt so as to have an easier walk. The thick fog of the morning had entirely covered the mountains. It disappeared in the afternoon, and we had fine weather until three o'clock, when we heard thundering in the distance which made me think that the storm was not far from us. However, I continued my journey until arriving at a small creek where I stopped to pass the night. My men had all the time necessary to prepare huts to shelter us before the storm reached us. The thunder was falling with terrible detonations which were echoed all round. Rain continued till half-past six in the evening, and the wind having changed to the east the fog soon attached itself to the tops of the mountains and before dusk they were covered from base to summit ...

On the 12th November, a thick fog with rainfall continued till 10 am. This very disagreeable weather having cleared up a little, I resumed my journey, passing through another chain of isolated mountains which may be nearly four miles in length, and sighting on the right the great range, the height of which is more and more considerable. All the soil of the ground I went over up to one o'clock in the afternoon appeared to be very rich. The hills are covered with kangaroos which resemble a flock of goats grazing peaceably, and offer to the eye a pleasing pastoral picture. I sowed four pumpkin seeds, which I happened to have on me, at the foot of the mountain, in a place denuded of bush, and also the stone of an apricot. I afterwards continued my journey, following the great range until I reached the bank of a creek, where I found a fire, and I could distinguish on the ground the footprints of a native and that of a child, who had but just left the place. I found a spear made of reed, which the little one had apparently left there, and with which the children are trained in the use of this weapon. There was some gum at one of its extremities in order to make that part heavier.

My attention was attracted by a mountain, which, although very high, appeared to me rather easy of access [probably Southern Peak or Tonalli Peak]. I resolved to ascend it with my men, convinced that from its summit I would be able to make a survey of the country around, which would enable me to form a judgment as to the direction in which I should have to go. I climbed that mountain easily enough for the first half-hour, allured by the singing of the pheasants, which I heard on all sides. Having reached a little over half the height, I met with a soil without consistency, like fine sand, interspersed with large and very sharp-edged stones, which made our march very disagreeable. These stones gave way under our feet and rolled down with a terrific noise. I was obliged, with my men, to open a narrow path, following, in single file, this passage among the stones and bushes, and sinking up to the knee in the sand, at the risk of having our legs broken by the stones, which were rolling, and which it was necessary to avoid by taking great precautions and stepping aside when we saw them come.

By this means I succeeded in ascending three-quarters of the height, where immense overhanging rocks, which seemed to be attached to nothing, offered an appalling scene. Enormous masses, on which we tried to hold ourselves in order to be able to pass, offered so little resistance that the slightest effort detached them, and some tumbled down under the pressure of our feet, when we found some large trees within our reach to hang on to. These masses in rolling down to the base carried away with them other rocks of various sizes with a thundering noise. When I happened to reach some large trees, generally blue-gum, I made my men rest, and during these stoppages I glanced at the plain from that great height with a feeling of admiration mingled with awe.

I continued to advance in that dangerous situation for half-an-hour, using my hands as well as my feet, which were bleeding. My aim was to reach the summit of the mountain, and I had deviated by only one hundred paces from my course. But I was literally stopped by a barrier of rocks which projected outwards in the shape of vaults, and which were pierced by various cavities, serving as a shelter to wild dogs and other wild animals …

When I arrived at the top of one of the hills which form the base of the mountain, Bungin, the mountaineer, saw a fire, and made a sign to me not to make any noise, and he stepped to the place where the fire was. Round it were seated some natives, who rose and put themselves on the defensive with their spears as soon as they perceived Bungin. He made another sign, inviting me to come with my troop, and began speaking, telling them not to be frightened; that he had come with Gogy to accompany us, and that we were travelling without any intention of doing them any harm. He told them to sit down again, which they did, after having questioned him and having observed us attentively.

The natives of this part of the country make use of a

weapon which is not employed by, and is even unknown to, the natives of Sydney. It is composed of a piece of wood in the form of a half circle, which they make as sharp as a sabre on both edges, and pointed at each end. They throw it on the ground or in the air, making it revolve on itself, and with such a velocity that one cannot see it returning towards the ground; only the whizzing of it is heard. When they throw it along the ground it is exactly like a cannon-ball, knocking down everything on its passage.

The manner in which the mountaineers receive the strangers is exactly the same as at Sydney, Parramatta and Hawkesbury. They have the same customs, the same way of living; their food consists of different species of kangaroos, opossums, squirrels, wild dogs, river and swamp fish and shells, lizard eggs (which they find in the sand on the banks of the rivers at a depth of one foot), large ant eggs, colo, or monkey (a species of opossum different from the others), wombat, serpents, lizards with red bellies, and other species, &c.,&c. Goondel's troop was well provided with opossums. They had also a wild dog, which they roasted in a hole after the style of the Hunter River natives. They appeared to be good hunters, and had five hounds with them.

The weapons of these natives, with the exception of the one mentioned previously, are of the same kind as those of the natives of Sydney. Their spears and clubs are similar; they all possess a small axe of English make, with which they catch various animals necessary to their subsistence. They wear a belt they make with opossum hair, plaited as thick as a pen-holder. It is composed of several of these plaits, and is about ten or twelve feet in length. They wear it very tight above the hips. It is used to hang their various instruments on, such as the axe, whamharha [woomera], whady, &c.

The natives here paint their face, arms, and thighs in the same way as those of Sydney, and they wear the same ornaments, with the addition of one composed of a part of the female kangaroo. The only difference consists in their mantles, which they make with the skins of various animals sewed together with sinews from the tail of the kangaroo;

but before sewing them they form various squares on the inside of the skin with the edgy part of a bivalve shell, which process makes the skin softer and easier to handle. When they have killed a kangaroo they always preserve the two middle teeth of the upper jaw, which are very long and of a beautiful and pure white when well cleaned. When they have a dozen they make a necklace of them, which is one of the principal ornaments of the women. They wear it on their forehead. They have another kind of necklace made of small reeds, and which they wear on their neck. This necklace goes seven or eight times round the neck, and they let a piece of at least six inches hang in the middle of their back. When they have only three or four teeth, and are not able to make a necklace, they stick them in their hair with gum, taking care that they come on the forehead or on the ears. Sometimes the men also adorn themselves with these necklaces, but they are contented with the reed ones, and stick the kangaroo teeth in their hair with gum. They, as well as some of the women, usually wear on their forehead a band of an oval shape, and red tinted, made as a net with opossum hair.

I had a fire lighted at once on the spot I had chosen for the present. I had my party seated, and whilst some soldiers were skinning the warring [small kangaroo or wallaby], I made Bulgin ask the natives the nearest place where water could be obtained. One of them rose instantly, and pointed with his hand to a place which contained some. Gogy, the native in my service, went near the mountaineers in nearly the same manner as Bungin, and held my gun in his hands to show them that he could make use of our arms; but nobody paid any attention to him except Wallarra, who was there, and knew him. He called him, and made him sit by his side. He was the only one who spoke to him. The others from time to time threw terrible glances at him, biting their lips, which did not augur very well for him, and made him aware of the danger he was running among them. He came back to me very angry, and told me that the chief of that tribe was called Goondel, and that one of them called Mootik was the only one who could give me any information about the new settlement which, he had heard, was on the other side of the mountains. Wallarra had told him to apply to that native, but, when asked, the latter did not answer the questions put to him on that subject, although Wallarra had told him that it was by my orders he questioned him, because it was my intention to examine this new settlement when I knew its location and the number of days required to reach it. Mootik had got up, looking at him with terrible eyes and biting his lips, and had gone to the place where the water was. When he had come back he seated himself near Goondel, spoke in his ear, and took an opossum which he had distributed among those present for their dinner, but offered none to him [Gogy], an omission he considered as the greatest insult.

He also told me that this chief had promised his daughter to Bungin, in order to retain him in his tribe; that the girl was called Wheengeewhungee, was very young, and that Bungin had accepted the offer, and had asked him to intimate to me that he would not follow me any farther.

While I was talking to Gogy our dinner had been prepared. I gave him his share, but he absolutely refused to touch it. He had his eyes constantly fixed on the place where the natives were, and did not miss one of their movements. Having asked him what prevented him from eating, and what made him look so sad, he answered that if I had any consideration for him I would go back. He was certain, he said, that if I spent the night on this spot, Goondel and his party would kill him.

I could not succeed in reassuring him, even by telling him that I would go a few miles farther to look for a suitable place to spend the night; that, besides, he had nothing to fear, certain as he was of my assistance and that of my troop; and that after this day I intended returning to the depot by another route to avoid meeting Goondel and his tribe. I expressed to him my surprise at seeing him possessed of so little courage, for he knew I had a sentry on watch during the night. All this failed to restore his confidence; but as he was absolutely necessary to me in making the huts for myself, my people, and the provisions at night, I could not let him leave without inconvenience. I, therefore, decided to go, and having had everything put in order, and everyone having taken his arms and utensils, I called Bungin, who at once came to me. He talked with Gogy for some time, and the latter told me that Bungin asked my permission to stop for this day with Goondel who was giving him his daughter, but that he would join me on the morrow before breakfast time. Having no reason to keep him back, I granted his request, hoping to get rid altogether of a mouth quite useless to me, and I made my people take the route to the depot.

Gogy was not long in perceiving that Mootik and one of the other mountaineers were following us at less than two hundred paces behind, and that they stopped every time we stopped. He noticed that they were well armed, and that they each had a spear fixed to the whamharha, which they usually employ to throw their spear with greater force when opportunity offers. I gave the order to proceed without seeming to take any notice of the natives. Gogy alone observed all their movements. He stopped when they were shouting, and told me that they were calling the others to help them. He looked as if he had lost his reason. My soldiers sometimes called him 'gevenet', which in the native language signifies coward, and he used then to get out of temper. After following us in that manner for more than one hour the two natives stopped, and after looking at us for some time, they retraced their steps. Gogy was the first to notice it, and made me aware of it with an expression of joy ...

On 13th November I continued my route to the depot, following the river in search of wild ducks. On arriving at the junction of the two rivers I heard the voice of a native who was calling, and having stopped my troop, I saw, a few minutes after, Bungin who was coming to me with a young native who had paid us a visit the evening before. Bungin told me that the girl who the chief had promised to him had taken to the woods, and they had not been able to find her, although they had looked for her during the whole of the afternoon on the 12th, and seeing that she could not be found he had left the natives, in order to rejoin me, after having

exchanged his spears and whamharha … for a few ornaments
he had received from the natives. He had taken the young
fellow with him because, as he had neither father nor mother,
he was not able to subsist without being helped. He added
that he had followed my footsteps until dusk, stopping near
the river, having only one opossum to share with his companion who was crying very much over the fatigue he had
experienced, and that, having seen our fire during the night,
he had left early in the morning to try to overtake us before
breakfast.

I had some food given to Bungin and the young native. They appeared as if they were in great need of it. I learnt
that Goondel and his tribe proposed to go up the river today
to try and find his bride. He told me also that he knew a
shorter way to go back to the depot, in ascending a mountain and passing several high hills which were on the other
side of the river, by which means we should reach the depot
before sunset …

On arriving at the depot I found there a kangaroo
weighing eighty pounds, which my men had killed, and they
hastened to make some soup for us with the tail and the head
of the animal, which comforted us and made us forget our
fatigue for a while. I learnt that Bulgin, one of the natives I
left at the depot with his two wives, had disappeared on the
day after my departure. On that day he had gone hunting
with some men from the depot and the young native who
had come with Wooglemai. He had told his wives to leave
some short time after him, pretend to look after ant nests,
and then to make for the woods. Bulgin, having given some
pretext to remain in the rear, the soldier had seen him run
out of his reach, and a short time afterwards having seen the
young native run away with his coat, had fired a shot over his
head. It frightened him so much that he let himself drop on
the ground, believing he was mortally wounded, and gave
time for the soldier to catch him and take him back to the
depot …

On the 14th November, being obliged to wait at the
depot for the return of the wagon, I made arrangements so as

to let my men have a rest, to make them recover from their fatigue, intending to send some of them kangaroo hunting on the morrow.

The natives are extremely indulgent to their offspring. Everything they may desire is granted at once to them—even the spears, and the mothers' necklaces, &c. I noticed that little Gogy used to take a sharp-pointed spear his father had made for him and thrust it in his mother's thighs more than one inch deep. The latter after having cried for some time then dressed her wounds, looked at her child in laughing, and told me her son would be a great warrior. He used to do the same thing to his father, and struck heavy blows with his club on his shoulders, taking all the attitudes of a combatant. The father, to encourage him, pretended to be vanquished, and asked for his mercy. The little one then, with an insulting air, told him to get up, and after having thrown two or three spears at him they made friends again.

Cruelty and laziness are two prominent characteristics of the natives. During their marches the women are obliged to carry the children, and have in addition a net in the form of a sack hanging on their back in which they have to carry opossums, and all tools necessary to their husbands, such as kangaroo bones, which they use as chisels, bivalve shells, which they employ for sharpening the point of their spears; and other utensils, as well as lines of various descriptions, gum, &c. They are in everything their husbands' beasts of burden. Should his wife not obey his first command the husband strikes her on the head with his club as a warning, and continues his route as if nothing out of the way had taken place. If his wife attempts to resist his orders he breaks her arm with blows from his club, thrusts spears in her thighs and other parts of the body, and thus compels her to obey. They have a strong inclination to steal one another's wives when opportunity offers, and they then change country in order to escape being pursued. When the wife of one of their enemies falls into their hands they drag her by force in the bush, holding her by the arms; and when she is covered with blood through the pricking of the brushes and nearly dying, they, whatever number there might be, commit all sorts of violence and brutalities upon her, after which the first one takes her for his wife; then the remainder of the troop is obliged to respect her as such, and she has to follow her new husband and obey him.

An unforeseen incident soon troubled our tranquillity, and gave rise to a very disagreeable quarrel. I had given to Gogy's child a few morsels of kangaroo left from my breakfast which he had taken to his mother's hut to eat. Unfortunately, this woman started eating a portion of this meat which she took from the child, who complained to his father, shouting and crying. The father having ordered his wife to let him alone, she could not resist taking some more pieces of the meat, which caused the child to renew his cries.

Gogy then took his club and struck his wife's head such a blow that she fell to the ground unconscious. My people having tried to appease him, he went out of the hut, dropped his club, and started abusing his wife, pacing in front of the hut. He soon started again with a four-pointed spear, which is used by the natives for fishing purposes, and thrust it several times in her thighs and several other parts of her body. He then ran to the pile of arms, and taking hold of a musket, aimed at his wife and would have shot her had not my men at once taken the musket out of his hands, telling him that he had no right to take arms which did not belong to him. This appeared to vex him very much. He then laid down near Bungin, who seemed to remonstrate with him and try to make him keep quiet.

After dinner, seeing that nobody was taking any notice of him, he got infuriated again, and again struck his wife on the head with his club, and he left her on the ground nearly dying, before Bungin, who was seated, could come to her assistance. He got up at once and succeeded in making her regain consciousness by throwing some water on her face. He afterwards sucked the wound she had on her head, bandaged it tightly with a handkerchief she happened to have, and made her lie down near the fire.

While Bungin was nursing this woman, Gogy was walking up and down in a great fury. Nobody dared to speak to him for fear he should again ill-treat his wife, who was in a pitiable state. At last he came to me and said he was almost certain one of my people had seduced his wife, and that he had determined to kill her if she did not tell him who it was that seduced her. I represented to him that the thing was impossible; that it was only the stage of anger in which he was that made him believe things which did not exist; and that should he kill this poor woman his child would have no one to suckle him. But it was all in vain. He told that he had determined to give his child to some people at Parramatta when he had killed the mother, and going back to his wife, mad with anger, he struck her a terrible blow on her shoulders, asking her to give him at once the name of her seducer; that should she persist in withholding that name from him, he would kill her on the spot. He intimidated her so much by his threats that she named Wittington, one of my soldiers, assuring him that she had never responded to his advances.

Gogy sat by his fire without uttering a word. He mended his spears, sharpening them again, biting his lips all the time.

This disagreeable day was spent in this manner until dusk, when fearing lest Gogy should commit some act of violence, I had a sentry told off to follow all his movements, and in the case of his perpetrating any excess, to fire upon him if there were no other means of restraining him. Gogy carried his cruelty so far as not to allow his wife to pass the night in his hut; he would not even light her fire, and she was obliged to lay in this pitiable state in the open air until daybreak.

Everything continued quiet during the night, and I had to satisfy the questions of the natives about the sentry (whom they never had seen before outside the hut at night) by telling them that it was to protect them against evil spirits. They performed in trembling their customary ceremonies, and went back to their hut …

15th November—Bungin dressed the unfortunate woman's wounds. She had an inflammation where she had been wounded by the spear. He bandaged her thigh very tightly a little above the wounds to prevent the inflammation spreading up. He made for that purpose a bandage with the bark of a small tree. He then examined the wound in the head, cleaned it with much patience and dexterity, washed it with cold water, and replaced the handkerchief as it was before. I witnessed this operation, and its effect on this unfortunate woman was very marked, for she was soon able to eat some rice and sugar I had given her.

I had decided to send some of my men kangaroo hunting with the natives, when Bungin came and told me that he was going with the child he had brought with him from Goondel to look for Bulgin, who had taken away the new axe I had given him, and after his departure I sent two men with the young native who Bungin had left, and who was obliged to stay with us against his will. He knew the country, and I was certain he would take my men to the places frequented by kangaroos. I was not deceived in my expectation. At about two o'clock I saw them coming back with a superb male weighing one hundred pounds. This was a good addition to our provisions ...

On 16th November, I sent two of my men hunting, and I told Gogy to go with them, but I could not induce him to leave his hut. He looked sorry for having ill-treated his wife, and was trying to make peace with her.

I myself left with two soldiers to reconnoitre the environs of the depot. I gathered a quantity of plants and I killed a small and very pretty bird; the head, the neck, and part of its body were red. When arriving at the depot I found the young native quarrelling with one of my men, who accused him of trying to steal the waist-coat of one of his comrades, and abandon him in the woods, where he certainly would have lost his way. I forbade my men molesting him in future, and they were reconciled ...

On the 17th November, I had the huts repaired where the rain found its way through; everybody worked at it so as to have it finished quickly. Afterwards I had our arms cleaned, and the whole day was spent in doing those two things. Gogy asked me to allow his wife to go away in the wagon when it came back, which I promised, for I greatly desired to get rid of him, as he had become useless to me since he had ill-treated his wife. He was now very affectionate to her. He would not go out of the hut under any pretence, not even to fetch the water he wanted. His anger had all gone, but he appeared to be jealous of his wife ...

Wooglemai had followed the wagon and had with him a young man, whom he called Badbury. They were well received by Gogy and his wife. I named this young native *Le Tonsure,* because he had lost some of his hair in falling head-long from his mother's arms into a fire. The skin of his head had been burnt, and the hair had not grown again on that part, which resembled a monk's tonsure. He only suffered from this in rainy weather, when the rain fell on his head, and he then covered it with some bark ...

A little before dusk, Gogy came and asked my per-mission to accompany his wife when the wagon left. I pre-tended to feel inclined to refuse acceding to his request, in order that he should be grateful for my granting it later on. He insisted very much on the necessity of his accompanying his wife and taking her to his father, saying that he could not trust anybody to do it. As I wanted to get rid of him I told him he could go, and it pleased him very much ...

On 23rd November I pursued the same route which I had taken while on my previous journey. My young natives fol-lowed without grumbling. They were accustomed to carry the haversack, the weight of which was diminishing in pro-portion as the provisions were being consumed. On arriving at the junction of the two rivers I perceived a fire on the opposite side, near the large river, and three natives seated under a tree with two women and some children who rose at once on seeing my troop, and who closely watched us.

My two young natives said we ought to stop for a while, because we could not go on without speaking to those natives, and, dropping their haversacks, they went to them. A short time afterwards they returned and told me they had learnt that Goondel, Mootik, and Wallarra had come to receive them. A little while after we saw these three natives cross the river on a waterfall in front of us, and they sat under the shade of a she-oak. Wallarra came last with a stick alight in his hand and a piece of kangaroo. After their fire had been lighted my two young natives went to them, and they were received without ceremony. Mootik gave them a leg of kangaroo, well dried by fire, and Wallarra a rib of the same animal boned and properly dried.

I had gone to the bank of the river to try to shoot some wild ducks, and when coming back the two young natives told me that Goondel, seeing I had no intention of doing any harm to them, was contemplating paying me a visit with his party, and I felt rather pleased about it. This was a proof of his confidence in me, which I decided to augment by presenting him with a new axe, hoping to get from him some particulars which would be of use to me while progressing into the interior. In consequence I had the dinner prepared to receive them; but in vain did I wait till 4 pm for them ...

My provisions were reduced to a small quantity of flour and some pickled pork, which would hardly be sufficient for our meals. Chance, however, favoured us in supplying us here with a good meal, one of my soldiers having shot an eel weighing twelve pounds, which he had found in the creek ...

At six o'clock I found myself at a distance of two miles from the western passage. I was obliged to climb over a very steep height, at the summit of which I found a cave large enough to contain twenty men. I was then at only half a mile from the passage, and I sent two men in order to discover it, instructing them to ascend the mountain at the north of this passage. The rain compelled me to seek a shelter for myself and my men in the cave which, the natives assured me, was the home of wombats. I waited till seven o'clock in the cave for my two men, who related to me that after passing the range which was in front of us we would enter an immense plain; that from the height where they were on the mountain they had caught sight of only a few hills standing here and there in this plain; and that the country in front of them had the appearance of a meadow.

On the faith of this favourable report, I continued my march until nightfall, climbing over a hill comparatively easy of access which led me to the mouth of the passage formed by a perpendicular cut in the mountain [Barrallier Pass, between Mount Meier and Myanga Mountain], the profiles of which, north and south, were of an immense height and presented to the eye a majestic aspect. On the sandy soil of this passage an infinite number of small traces made by the wild beasts could be seen …

On 26th November, at daybreak, I left with two men to verify by myself the configuration of the ground, and to ascertain whether the passage of the Blue Mountains had really been effected. I climbed the chain of mountains north from us, and when I had reached the middle of this height [Mount Moogan], the view of a plain as vast as the eye could reach confirmed to me the report of the previous day …

I was running short of provisions and I was not expecting any by the return of the wagon. I decided to go to meet it, and to send it back to Parramatta, with an order for fresh provisions; or, should I miss it on my way, to proceed to Parramatta and see to the sending of provisions myself … I advanced, following the traces of the wheels of the wagon, and towards noon I took a rest on the banks of a creek. A little while after I heard the report of a gun, a circumstance which filled me with joy, as I was persuaded it could only have been fired by the drover of the wagon. I resumed my march at once, and after half-an-hour had elapsed my two young natives saw the escort, and a moment after came to tell me that Gogy and his child were there … I made Gogy build a hut to shelter the effects which were in the wagon, and I established myself there for the night, taking care to use the barrel of rum as a pillow, fearing the indiscretion of my men.

In my hurry, when I left the depot I had forgotten to take the thermometer, and I was sorry of that circumstance, which precluded me from giving the degree of heat of this part of the country.

On the 5th December I sent the wagon away, escorted by four men, to whom I gave my two young natives as guides, and whose orders were to bring back some provisions. I decided I would wait for their return, giving them express instructions to be back as quickly as they possibly could, as I was willing to attempt for the third time to find a passage across the Blue Mountains by following the second river, which, it appeared to me, came from the south-west. I wrote about this intention to His Excellency, who, in his letters, always recommended me to the perseverance which was so necessary to the journey I had undertaken.

After the wagon had gone I went hunting with Gogy. I saw several kangaroos, but they were too shy for us to be able to shoot them. I came back at eleven o'clock with empty hands. The men who had been sent to try and catch the cattle, and who had left here early in the morning, returned in the evening very tired and unsuccessful. They told me they had met a bull which was very lame from a wound inflicted by a spear thrown at him by some native defending himself, and which it still had in its side. This spear came three or four feet out of the side of the poor animal, and formed an acute angle with its legs …

On the 8th December we had southern wind, and the rain fell continually till 4.30 pm. I went with Gogy in search of opossums, accompanied by his wife and child, who, on the way, were looking for the nests of large ants, the eggs of which they eat greedily. These ants are very large and very plucky. They defend their habitations with an incredible obstinacy. Their sting causes a sharp pain, which lasts for a long time, and the natives take great care to protect their legs against it as much as they can. If they are hit with a switch they rush to it and bite it; and if they are pursued, they bite it while retreating, facing their aggressor all the time.

I travelled the plain for a while, and Gogy, having

detected on the trunk of a tree the fresh traces of an opossum, climbed it and caught two very large ones. He threw one down after he had killed it, but the other gave him more trouble. He was obliged to enlarge the hole where it was, and to draw it out with a crooked stick. He then threw it down alive and I shot it dead when, in trying to escape, it was climbing another tree. The two opossums were the only articles of food I could procure on that day. The wind kept to the south.

On the 9th December, rain and thundering all day long. The large branches of the trees under which our huts were standing were quite rotten, and in falling, exposed us to the danger of being crushed under them. At 6 pm a wild dog came at a short distance from our huts. My greyhound chased and overtook it, but it came back after having given and received a few bites.

On the 10th December, the weather having changed for the better, I sent two men hunting whilst I occupied myself with looking for plants. My hunters returned at ten o'clock with a young kangaroo, which was of great help, as we were absolutely short of food. I had part of it prepared for our dinner, and arranged for the rest to be preserved for cases of need.

About 4 pm I saw a native coming. Gogy went to welcome him, and after a short conversation, they came and sat by my side. I learnt from this native that Kelly had passed at Manhangle in the morning, accompanied by two men and one horse loaded with provisions, and that they had shot at them several times. He told me that himself and Wooglemai, whom I knew, were the only men in his party, the rest being women and children. They had been obliged to run away, and one bullet passed very near his shoulders. Having seen my camp, he had come to make his complaint to me. When he had finished speaking, he took his net and gave me several swamp shells, which I liked very much. I gave him, in return, a joint of kangaroo, which he ate, and, picking up his axe and his net, he returned whence he had come.

It is not of any advantage, but, on the contrary, it is

very dangerous, to offer any insult to the natives. They avenge themselves of it sooner or later, and the first white man they meet without means of defence becomes their victim. They make use of the most cruel tortures on the one they can catch, whoever he might be, without troubling in the least about enquiring whether he belonged or not to the party who ill-treated them.

The weather was fair today and the heat moderate.

On the 11th December, thinking the wagon would very likely cross the river in the morning, I went with Gogy and two of my men to meet it. When I arrived at Manhangle I directed my march towards a fire I had caught sight of, and when I was thirty paces from it, the native pointed out to me a big wild dog lying in a bush. I thought that if I hid myself I would be able to shoot it, but my greyhound had just perceived it, and running to it they started fighting. They fought for a while, then my dog let it go at a great distance from me.

Gogy told me that the fire I had reached by that time had been lighted by the native who had come to complain the day before. I saw several natives on the bank opposite Manhangle, who, recognising Gogy, called him. He went to them after giving his new axe to his wife. He told me he would come to meet me at Barhagal.

On 12 December, I sent the soldiers back under the guidance of a native, and I left with Gogy, his wife, and her brother, a very intelligent boy, who insisted upon following me. After crossing the large creek, at about six o'clock, I met a superb black ox, which looked at me, without being frightened. I chased it, and it disappeared in the scrub.

Gogy set the country over which we were passing on fire to avenge ourselves on the natives who had burnt our huts. I arrived at the second creek at 5.30, where I found my huts burnt, and I continued to walk till 7.30 so as to get to the third creek, where I settled for the night. I discovered here several traces of the natives who had passed with the women and the children on the previous day, and who seemed to have directed their steps towards our depot. I feared they might have molested the people I had left there, and this thought made me very uneasy …

I started early on the morning of the 13th December. As before, I found my huts had been burnt, and I was at the depot at nine o'clock … I heard from a man in the depot, who had gone hunting on the 12th, that he had met seven natives, who had stopped at a gunshot from him. He was then pursuing a big kangaroo, which on seeing the natives had stopped, turning its back on my man, who, having come nearer, placed himself behind a tree, and shot at the animal which fell with a hind-leg broken. This had rid him of the natives, who when they had heard the detonation, and seen the kangaroo fall, had taken to their heels, uttering great shouts.

While I was away, the people at the depot lighted every night a large fire in front of the huts, and retired in some bush fifty paces behind, always having a sentry on duty to warn them in case any natives came. By this means they were insured against any surprise, and would have been able to easily disperse the natives without these latter even seeing them. At nine o'clock in the evening, after having given the orders for the night, and placed the sentry at his post, I had some rum distributed to each of my men, and made them retire to their huts …

On the 14th December the fog which cleared off about ten in the morning was replaced by very fine weather, and I sent the wagon back with the [sick soldier] and two men. I gave them Gogy's brother-in-law as a guide. I had had great trouble in persuading the latter to leave his sister, of whom he was very fond. I only decided him by giving him a soldier's vest.

After the wagon had gone I made my men clean their arms, and I got everything prepared for my departure. I limited to six the number of those who were to accompany me. I felt nearly certain of being successful this time, by following the [Wollondilly] river, the source of which must be in the mountains, which I could not reach.

Gogy told me that by following that river I would enter the territory of a tribe who do not use the whamharha.

Their spears are much longer than those belonging to the natives of these countries, and they are made from branches of trees which they straighten with fire. These natives cannot throw their spears to a great distance, on account of the way they hold them. He also told me they were anthropophagi [cannibals], and that we ought not to try and mix with them, because they would play us some nasty trick …

On the 15th December I went away with my six men, leaving three well-armed soldiers at the depot. I told Gogy to follow me. I had persuaded him to leave his wife at the depot, and we had already proceeded two miles in the gorge, following a direction S.70 degrees 0', when we heard a woman's shouts. It was Gogy's wife, who would not, she said, stay at the depot with strangers. This incident put me to the inconvenience of having this woman and her child at my train, and I still continued marching in the gorge. On arriving at the first river the woman was exhausted, and I was obliged to halt near the water. Whilst dinner was being prepared I saw the country a mass of flames towards the north-east, at about five miles from us, near the mountains.

Gogy told me it was Goondel who, with his party, was hunting bandicoots, lizards, snakes, kangaroo rat, &c. and that we must not disturb him. I saw he was frightened. I reassured him by saying that my intention was not to follow the banks of this river where we were, but to cross over to the other side after dinner in order to continue our march as far as my old quarters, where I expected we would spend the night. I did not want to hurry, as I had plenty of time to arrive there. I told him he need not be afraid at night, because I had my greyhounds, which would warn us should some strangers come. This way of reasoning appeared to satisfy him.

When at about three o'clock I was proceeding forward I was astonished to see Gogy with his child upon his shoulders marching in front. This was an indication that he would soon leave me. We arrived in the evening at my old quarters, where I found my huts had been pulled down. Gogy put them up again. He closed one of their openings with branches from the trees, and he made a bed for himself by the fireside with the bark of tea-tree, which is very soft. The heat was excessive during the whole day. The thermometer— in the morning, 70 degrees 30'; at noon, 93 degrees 20'; at 4 o'clock, 92 degrees 50'; in the evening 76 degrees 0'; southern wind, sky cloudy.

On the 16th December, Gogy came and told me that his wife not being able to follow us, he was obliged to go back to the depot with her. It was but an excuse. The fact was that, being on the territory of Goondel, he was afraid of falling into the hands of that chief. Gogy had told me long before my journey into the mountains that he had been obliged to fly to Goondel's to escape being punished for an offence he had committed. Goondel had kept him and hidden him, providing for all his wants with the greatest friendship. After he had stayed with him for a long time he left him to go to his people, whose anger had abated, and, after having submitted himself to the usual punishment, he was well received, and nobody made any allusion to the past. Unfortunately, having made an incursion with a friend of his, a great enemy of Goondel's, they had met a woman of this chief's tribe in the neighbourhood of Nattai. His friend pursued her, caught her, and, after having perpetrated upon her the usual brutalities, he killed her, and, having tied her to a tree, they cut off some of her flesh, which they grilled and ate. He suspected that Goondel had discovered he had taken a part in the murder of his sister, and he was certain that he would not spare him should he succeed in seizing him. He kept continually on his guard and well armed when he was compelled to travel in his territory. I allowed him to go, and continued my march to the second river …

After progressing for four miles towards S.24 degrees E., the composition of the soil changed, and became a kind of whitish clay, covered with small pebbles, and absolutely bad. The trees were blue-gum, yellow-gum, ironbark, mahogany, &c. At noon I came in front of a mountain very remarkable on account of its pyramidal form. I shot a few wild ducks, which were the only game I could get. I then took a sketch of the country, and resumed my march, stopping my troop at one o'clock for dinner.

It was about two o'clock when I perceived a great volume of smoke coming from the west. I sent some men to ascertain where it was coming from, but I could not obtain any particulars. The men I had sent returned very tired, and told me that after having ascended and descended several hills they had come to the base of the mountains, and that they had seen the smoke issuing from the other side of the range.

I resumed my march at 3.30 in the afternoon, going round various hills denuded of trees, which take rise in the mountains and slope down to the banks of the river nearly at right angles. The fallen rocks and the precipices offered obstacles very difficult to surmount. The falls are caused by torrents coming from the mountains. The astonishing ravages they make are evidenced by the large number of uprooted gigantic trees one sees there, and by the enormous rocks rolled down into the very bed of the river.

I saw another column of smoke towards west-north-west, but I could not ascertain whether it was caused by the natives or some volcano. I was surrounded with mountains on all sides, the only passage I had being the banks of the river, which were often almost inaccessible. Besides, the more I advanced the more the river trended towards the south, and this fact left me no hope of being able to cross the mountains. I was simply following their bases, which had the appearance of a multitude of pyramids or cones, standing like as many detached sugar-loaves placed on top of one another. Even supposing I could overcome all these obstacles, I would arrive at a chain of mountains the direction of which is about north and south, and the height of which, compared to that of the sugar-loaves, is immense. This chain of mountains, which is the one I had passed on the 23rd November, could only be ascended by making almost superhuman efforts.

I discovered at various places indications which left no doubt as to this country being inhabited, or at all events frequently visited by the natives. From their own reports,

Accident on the Road at Victoria Pass
by William Romaine Govett (watercolour, c.1835)

Bushwalker crossing billabong of Nattai River

Nattai River valley

Cascades, Kanangra Creek

Kanangra Walls

they assemble there when they make incursions into enemies'
territory, or when some troubadour comes with his party to
sing and teach them a new song. This is a custom which
seems to have extended even to these regions.

I arrived in Sydney after three days' hard walking, and the
kind reception extended to me by His Excellency quite com-
pensated me for all my hardships, and, to some extent, con-
soled me for having failed in the accomplishment of what I
had planned, viz., going over the Blue Mountains by the
route I had thought of.

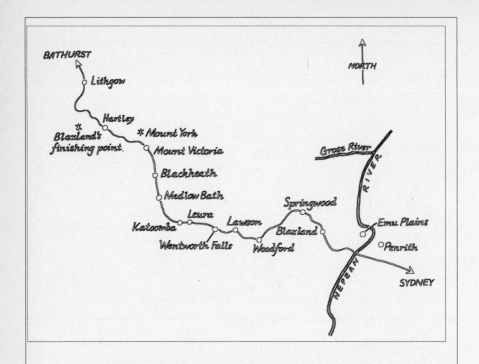

Map 2: GREAT WESTERN HIGHWAY
the approximate route of Blaxland, Wentworth and Lawson

II

Gregory Blaxland

The insurmountable barrier

In 1813 the thirty-five-year-old free settler Gregory Blaxland, William Wentworth and Lieutenant William Lawson found a way across the Blue Mountains. The party had no leader, and included servants and convicts. There are two points of particular interest about its achievement.

The first is that, according to historian Chris Cunningham, they were not the first white men to do so. Former convict John Wilson, who spent years living with Aborigines, probably reached the upper Cox's River, although not necessarily by the same route taken by Blaxland's party, by 1798. The second point of interest is that Blaxland's journey actually terminated in fairly mountainous countryside. Mount Blaxland, where his expedition turned back, lies to the west of the Great Western Highway after the Jenolan Caves turnoff, if one is heading away from Sydney. It's fairly rough country a long way from the Bathurst plains, which makes Blaxland's claim to have seen 'forest land all around … sufficient to feed the stock of the colony … for the next thirty years' hard to understand.

The western plains were reached later in 1813 by the government surveyor, George Evans, whom Governor Mac-

quarie sent in Blaxland's footsteps. Evans was followed by
Cox, who in 1815 completed the road across the Blue Mountains, subsequently the site of townships such as Leura and
Katoomba, along the path taken by Blaxland's party. In 1814
Macquarie was to praise the three explorers for 'their
enterprizing and arduous exertions on the tour of discovery'
and give them each four hundred hectares of land beyond the
mountains. Blaxland, a querulous man, never considered the
reward adequate.

The following account was written by Blaxland in
the third person (except for one lapse, when he is boasting of
his own marksmanship) and published in 1823. It is clearly
the work of a restless man of action rather than a man of
words, and the following version has been heavily edited and
cut. Nevertheless, it is one of the prime records of Australian
exploration—even if the outward trip took only three weeks.

The pile of stones found by the explorers on 19 May
has been attributed variously to Bass, Caley and Hacking. Its
original position, like its builder, is now unknown. The present
replica, known as Caley's Repulse, was built in 1912.
The Emu Island in the Nepean River Blaxland refers to no
longer exists.

The account is preceded by Blaxland's own explana-
tion, from a letter he wrote in 1819, of his motivation for
making the crossing. This too is in the third person.

———

He arrived in the colony in the year 1806, after which he
entered into a large business principally connected with the
grazing and breeding of cattle and sheep … Soon after that
period he found that the stock kept amongst the farms in the
more cultivated parts of the country near the coast did not
do so well as might have been reasonably expected, which
induced him to remove part of them farther into the interior,
over the south creek where some of them were before stationed, by which step the different flocks and herds had an
almost unlimited scope of pasturage between the south creek

and the Nepean River in a fine grazing country. But even
there he found that great part of the grass when hard fed died
away, and that the pasturage in a little time became much less
productive, particularly where the ground was close fed and
highly manured, and new establishments of stock and farms
for the purpose of cultivation formed around in every direction.

[This] occupied the land and daily circumscribed the
limits the stock [had] at first enjoyed, so much so that in one
season soon after their first establishment, when the caterpil-
lars destroyed the grass in an unusual manner, there was not
for a long time sufficient food for them in the whole space
between the creek and the river ... They began to fall off,
which circumstance induced him to believe that without any
further increase in the stock he should be compelled by necessity to remove them in a few years, or submit to great loss
... He did not know of any unoccupied space of good pasturage on this side of the mountains by any means adequate
to the purpose.

Being fully convinced of the necessity of finding out
a further extension of pasturage, he made every enquiry in
his power respecting the practicability of discovering a passage over the Blue Mountains, but could at no time gain any
information to encourage or induce him to think that such
an undertaking was practicable. Mr. Caley and every other
person who had attempted it, or that knew any thing of the
country, described it as impossible, and asserted that the Blue
Mountains must inevitably remain an insurmountable barrier to the extension of the settlement.

Tuesday, May 11th, 1813.
Mr. Gregory Blaxland, Mr. William Wentworth and Lieutenant Lawson, with four servants, five dogs and four horses
loaded with provisions, ammunition and other necessaries,
took their departure to endeavour to explore the interior of
the country, and to effect a passage over the Blue Mountains

between the western river and the River Grose. They crossed
the Nepean River at the ford on to Emu Island at four o'clock
in the afternoon and proceeded by their calculation two miles
through forest land and good grass, encamped at five o'clock
at the foot of the first ridge of the mountains ...

Wednesday, May 12th, 1813.
They proceeded on their journey at nine o'clock in the morning, when the heavy dew was well off, and ascended the first
ridge of the mountains; fell in with a large lagoon of good
water full of very coarse rushes; saw the high land of Grose
Head bearing north by east about seven miles distance. They
proceeded this day about three miles and a quarter. The land
they passed over [was] covered with scrubby brush, very thick
at places, with some trees of ordinary timber. Most ... of the
way [there were] deep rocky gullies on each side of them. In
the evening they encamped at the head of a deep gully, which
they had to descend for water; found but just enough for the
night in a hole in the rock. The horses travelled very awk-
wardly, being much incommoded by the small trees and brush
at places, and [by] the ridge they followed being very crooked
and intricate between the gullies. A small patch of grass supplied the horses for the night. When they stopped they found
a kangaroo just killed by an eagle at the hole of water ...

Thursday, May 13th, 1813.
They found it impossible to travel through the brush before
the dew was off. At nine o'clock they loaded their horses
and proceeded a short distance, about a mile, and came into
a large tract of forest land, rather hilly. They computed it at
two thousand acres, the grass and timber tolerably good. This
forest land, they expect, reaches near to Grose Head in the
same direction with the river. Here they found a tract [track]
marked by a European by cutting the bark of the trees, and
several native huts at different places. When they had proceeded about two miles their course was stopped by a brush
much thicker than they had met with before. They altered
their course and endeavoured to find out another passage to

the westward; found every ridge they tried ending in a deep rocky precipice; came back to the thick brush they before left, which appeared [to be] the main leading ridge, determined to cut their way through it the next day; encamped in the forest land with plenty of good grass and water. Some of the horses, whilst waiting to explore the different points of the hill, fell several times with their loads, and dogs killed a large kangaroo this day ...

Friday, May 14th, 1813.
They left their camp at half-past nine o'clock in charge of two men ... to cut a way through the brush for the loaded horses to pass. This day they first began to make their track by cutting some of the bark of the trees on two sides. [They] cut a path through a very thick brush, about five miles, on what they considered to be the main ridge of the mountains between the western [Warragamba] river and the River Grose, keeping the heads of the gullies, which they supposed emptied themselves into the River Grose, on the right hand as they ascended the mountain. The gullies became much deeper and more rocky on each side of them. They returned to their camp at five o'clock.

Saturday, May 15th, 1813.
They left their camp as the day before in charge of the two men at half past nine o'clock; cut about two miles on the same ridge, found no food for the horses the whole of the way [and] returned to their camp at five o'clock. This day they lost much time in walking twice over the tract they had cut and marked the day before. Heard an emu on the other side of the gully calling continually in the night.

Sunday, May 16th, 1813.
They rested this day and arranged their future plan of proceeding. [Blaxland's note regarding this day of rest: 'A bad plan, it gave the men time to consider their danger and it was doubtful for some time next morning if they would proceed any further.' This was the sixth day of their expedition.]

The dogs killed two small kangaroos; one of the horses got away in the night, for which they pulled and tied in bundles a large quantity of grass ready for the next day. The dogs barked and ran off continually the whole of the night. At daylight they heard a most tremendous howling of native dogs, which appeared to have been watching them the whole of the night.

Monday, May 17th, 1813.
They found the horse that got away about a mile and a half back upon the tract they [had come up]. At nine o'clock loaded their horses with as much grass as they could lay on, besides their other loads, and proceeded by the track they had cut through the brush and marked the two preceding days, about six miles and a half … In the afternoon they encamped between two very deep gullies on a narrow ridge of the mountain [Linden], where they were forced to fetch water up the precipice they suppose six hundred feet or more … They could get scarcely enough [water] for the men—the horses went without this night [yet] performed their journey well throughout the day, not being forced to stand under their loads from any delay …

Tuesday, May 18th, 1813.
They left their camp as before and proceeded at nine o'clock to mark and cut a passage for the horses through the brush. Returned to their camp very tired and out of spirits.

Wednesday, May 19th, 1813.
They got ready by half past nine o'clock, and proceeded about a mile and a half in the track they had cut and marked the day before, along a very narrow ridge not more than fifteen or twenty yards over, with a very deep rocky precipice on each side … From this ridge they first began to have an extensive view of the settlements below.

At a little distance from the spot they ascended they found a heap of stones piled up in the shape of a pyramid by some European, one side of which the natives had opened

[as] if apparently to see if any thing was deposited in the middle. This they conjectured … to have been the end of Mr. Bass's track, who attempted some time back to pass the mountains and penetrate the interior. He piled up a heap of stones at the end of his journey, returned and reported it impossible to find a passage even for a person on foot.

They encamped [between Linden and Woodford] to refresh their horses at the head of a swamp covered with coarse rushy grass, with a run of good water through the middle of it. In the afternoon they left their camp and marked and cut a road for the next day. One of the horses fell this day with his load. Here they expected they had penetrated as far as any European before them …

Thursday, May 20th, 1813.
They got ready at nine o'clock and proceeded about four miles and three quarters; encamped at twelve o'clock at the head of a swamp of about three acres covered with rushy coarse grass with water running through the middle of it. The horses by necessity lived on the coarse swamp grass or rush [as] nothing else could be got for them.

They left the camp as before in the middle of the day, and marked and cut a road for the next day; [traces] of scarcely any animal and few birds to be seen; the ridge of the mountain wider here and more rocky, covered with brush and small crooked timber, with a small swamp clear of trees at the heads of the different streams of water which run down the side of the mountain [probably between Hazelbrook and Lawson].

One man dangerously ill with a cold …

Saturday, May 22nd, 1813.
They found all the horses fast in the morning [and] supposed it was a native the dogs drove off in the night. At nine o'clock they loaded their horses and proceeded in the tract they had marked rather more than three miles. When they reached the summit of the third and highest ridge of the mountains southward of Mount Banks, from the bearings of Prospect Hill and Grose Head, they computed this spot eighteen miles in a

straight line, from the river when they crossed. On the top of the mountain they found about two thousand acres of land clear of trees [King's Tableland, just south of Wentworth Falls], covered with loose stones and short coarse grass, much like some commons in England.

They proceeded about a mile and a half over the heath, and encamped by the side of a fine stream of water, with just enough wood for their fire, on one side of it. From the top of the mountain they had a fine view of all the settlements and country eastward, and of a great extent of country to the westward and south west, but their progress was stopped either westward or south-west by an impassable cliff of rocks, which appeared to divide the interior from the coast as with a stone wall rising immediately perpendicular, out of the side of the mountains.

In the afternoon they left their camp and horses in charge of three men and endeavoured to get down the precipice, [to] the earth below, by following some of the streams of water, or at some of the projecting points where the rocks had fallen down upon the earth on the side of the mountain, but they were disappointed in every attempt. In some places they conjectured the rocks rose a thousand feet perpendicular above the earth. Below here they expected, if they could have got down, to have procured specimens of the different stones and minerals of the country, as the stratas of the earth appear to have been exposed for many hundred feet from the top of the rocks to the beds of the different rivers which appeared to run below.

Here they saw the broken rocky country to the western side of the Cowpastures, all which country appears to have been formerly an earthquake or some dreadful Convulsion of Nature ... They returned to their camp very much disappointed from the appearance of the country below; it appeared to them sand and small scrubby bushes, intersected at places with broken rocky mountains, with streams of water running between each, eastward, to one point where they suppose they form the western river and enter the mountains. This day they were greatly in hopes they had surmounted half the difficulties they might have to encounter, expecting they might find a passage down more to the northward ...

Sunday, May 23rd, 1813.
They got ready at nine o'clock and proceeded about three miles and a half; they met with much difficulty with the horses. When they got out of the open land, the track not being marked and cleared at one o'clock, they encamped on the side of a swamp with a beautiful stream of water running through the middle of it [Jamison Creek]. They left their camp in charge of two men and proceeded to mark and clear a tract for the next day, which they found by experience the much readiest way of proceeding, although they had to walk all the ground twice over ...

Monday, May 24th, 1813.
They got ready at nine o'clock and proceeded about four miles and a half; encamped at twelve o'clock at the head of a swamp [between Medlow Bath and Blackheath]. They left their camp as before in the afternoon and proceeded to clear and mark a tract for the next day; returned at five o'clock this day. They again saw the country below them between ten and eleven o'clock—when the clouds ascended. They heard a native chopping very near them; as they were marking their road he ran away before he could be discovered; the dogs frightened him and appeared to run after him for some distance ...

Tuesday, May 25th, 1813.
They got ready at half past nine o'clock, and proceeded three miles and a half; encamped at two o'clock, on the side of a swamp. They left their camp as before, and proceeded to clear and mark a road for the next day—they were very much tormented this day, the under brush being prickly and full of small thorns; returned to their camp at five o'clock. Saw the track of the woombat the first time this day ...

Wednesday, May 26th, 1813.
They got ready about nine o'clock and proceeded about two
miles and three quarters; encamped at the head of a swamp;
left their camp in the afternoon and marked and cleared a
road for the next day. The brush continued still thorny; they
returned to their camp; at six o'clock the land to the westward appeared to them sandy and barren [Megalong and,
later, Kanimbla valleys; actually moderately good grazing
country]. This day they saw the fires of the natives below; by
the number they computed they amounted to, in all, about
thirty men, women and children. Saw more track of the
woombat ...

Thursday, May 27th, 1813.
They got ready about nine o'clock and proceeded about five
miles and a quarter, part of the way over another piece of
clear land without trees; encamped at one o'clock by the side
of a swamp; left the camp and marked a road as before; returned at five o'clock. They saw more natives' fires, about the
same number ... [probably near Mount Victoria]. They saw a
large piece of land below clear of trees, conjectured it to be a
poor reedy swamp. They met with some good timber for
building in this day's track ...

Friday, May 28th, 1813.
They got ready about nine o'clock and proceeded about five
miles and three quarters. Not being able to find water, they
did not encamp until five o'clock, when they encamped on
the edge of the precipice [the edge of Mount York] and discovered to their great satisfaction what they had considered
sandy and barren land below the mountains to be forest land,
covered with trees and good grass. In the evening they got
their horses down the mountain, when they again tasted grass
for the first time since they left the forest land on the other
side of the mountains ... found water about two miles below
the foot of the mountain [the River Lett]. The second camp
of natives moved before them about three miles. They passed
some timber fit for building in this day's track ...

Saturday, May 29th, 1813.

They fetched up the horses and began to descend the mountain [Mount York] at seven o'clock, through a pass in the rocks about thirty feet wide [which] they had discovered the day before, when the want of water made them more alert. Going down, they were forced to unload the horses part of the way and carry their loads themselves, as they could but just keep their footing without a load. Here a road for a cart might be easily made by cutting a trench slanting along the side of the mountain in the earth which lays against it, and which at this place joins the earth on the top. They computed this pass to be about twenty miles north-west in a straight line from the place where they ascended the mountain.

They reached the foot about nine o'clock and proceeded about two miles, most of the way through open meadow land clear of trees [and] covered with grass two and three feet high. They encamped on the bank of a fine stream of water [the River Lett] to rest themselves and to refresh their horses. The natives moved before them as the day before; the timber appeared rotten and not a sort for building. The dogs killed a kangaroo, which was very acceptable, they having lived on salt meat since they got the last …

Sunday, May 30th 1813.

They rested this day; shot a kangaroo 175 yards distance with my rifle. They found the climate very different from either the top of the mountains or the settlement on the other side, where when they left it the winter had not set in, nor any frost made its appearance. Here this night the frost covered the ground very thick and froze the leg of a kangaroo quite through … From the dead appearance of the grass, which turned brown and looked like sand at a distance, the frost must have been very very severe for some time past. They saw the track of the emu at several places near this camp.

Monday, May 31st, 1813.

They loaded their horses at nine o'clock and proceeded through the forest land, remarkably well watered, about six

miles; saw several kangaroos; went through many open meadows, clear of trees [and] covered with high good grass; crossed
two fine streams of water [River Lett and Cox's River]. This
day they came on some natives' fires, which they had left the
day before. They appeared to have been very busy sharpening
their spears, from the shavings and pieces of sharp stones they
had left behind. They appear on this side of the mountains to
have no huts nor to … climb the trees like the natives on the
other side. The only remains of food they had left round
their fireplaces was the flower of the honey suckle tree, which
grows like a bottle brush and [is] very full of honey, which
they had sucked out.

They encamped by the side of a very fine stream of
water [probably Lowther Creek, a tributary of the Cox's River]
a short distance from a high hill in the shape of a sugar loaf
[Mount Blaxland]. They left their camp in the afternoon and
ascended to its top, which terminated their journey; from
which place they saw forest land all around them sufficient to
feed the stock of the colony, in their opinions, for the next
thirty years …

Mr. Blaxland and one man nearly lost the party by
going after a kangaroo too far.

Tuesday, June 1st, 1813.
They got ready at nine o'clock and proceeded back to the
foot of the mountain, at the place where they came down,
and encamped, their provisions being nearly expended, their
clothes and shoes in particular worn out, and all of them ill
with bowel complaints, which determined them to return
home by the track they came … [They had] no doubt but
that they had effectually accomplished the object of their journey and that all the difficulties were surmounted which had
hitherto prevented the interior of the country from being
explored and the colony further extended …

III

Henry Anthill

The naming of parts

In late 1814 William Cox, a magistrate and private contractor at Hawkesbury, was awarded the job of building a road across the mountains. In six months his convict workers—who were rewarded with their freedom—built a road at least four metres wide and 170 kilometres long, from the Nepean to the Macquarie rivers, with over a dozen wooden bridges along its length. It was a good road, apart from the descent from Mount York. This was so steep that carriages would tie tree trunks behind them, to drag on the ground and act as a brake.

Major Henry Anthill accompanied Governor Lachlan Macquarie on his 1815 crossing of the mountains to inspect the new road and examine the land to the west. Lest the concern for personal comfort shown in the following account suggest its author was a fop, it ought to be pointed out that he was a war hero, and had been severely wounded carrying the colours at the storming of Seringapatam, in India, in 1799.

Tuesday, April 25, 1815.

This being the day fixed on by his Excellency the Governor for commencing his tour over the Blue Mountains to visit a new tract of country lately discovered, to the westward of them, left Sydney at half-past six o'clock in the morning, in company with Dr. Redfern ... and arrived at Parramatta at half-past eight. The morning cool and pleasant prepared breakfast for the Governor and Mrs. Macquarie, who arrived in their travelling carriage about an hour after. Our baggage carts, five in number, had been sent off from Sydney some days before, and had been directed to cross the River Nepean and await our arrival at the first depot ... At nine o'clock retired to rest. There being more guests than a small farm house could conveniently accommodate, beds could not be provided for all; I therefore got the cushions of the carriage, and with my boat cloak, lay down before a good fire, and slept soundly till morning.

Wednesday, April 26

Got up at daylight, and as I had not taken off my clothes, was soon ready to move, which, however, we did not do till seven o'clock. Sir John Jamison, who had been invited by the Governor to make one of his party, had requested we would breakfast at his farm, which we had promised to do, and arrived there about eight o'clock, distance of six miles from Mrs. King's. We found Mr. Secretary Campbell, Mr. Oxley, Surveyor-General, Mr. Meehan, his deputy, Sir John and his breakfast waiting for us. Sir John's farm being situated on the banks of the Nepean, the horses and carriage were sent round to the ford while we were at breakfast, about a mile down the river, where they crossed and came up to the Government stockyard opposite to Sir John's, and after allowing them a sufficient time to rest and take some corn, we all crossed in a boat, and at eleven o'clock started from Emu Plains, proceeding westward and along the plain till we came to the third mile tree. The ascent of the first range of mountains begins here. The country is much like that around Sydney, but larger and better timbered. About five and a half miles, came to the first depot established by Mr. Cox, when making the road, as a place of safety for his provisions for his working party. A small guard of soldiers are stationed here in a good log hut with two rooms, one of which answers as a store. It is placed about one hundred yards on the right of the road, near a small lagoon of fresh water. The soldiers had enclosed a small piece of ground for a garden, and one of them had displayed some taste in laying it out in little arbours and seats formed from the surrounding shrubbery, which gave the place an appearance of comfort and simplicity. After riding seven and a half miles further, we arrived about three o'clock at our first encampment, the road tolerably good the whole way from Emu Ford, mostly a gentle ascent. We found all our baggage, caravans, and servants safely arrived before us, and drawn up in regular order to receive us, which they did with three cheers.

Our dinner being ready and a table spread in the open air, we soon sat down to partake of it, and enjoyed our meal very much. After dinner served out a dram of rum to every man, which they were to receive every day, and all appeared happy and contented. After tea, took a short distance in the woods to enjoy the novelty of the scene around me, and, this being our first encampment, it may not be amiss to describe our situation. We were encamped in an extensive forest of large, lofty trees, mostly of stringy and iron bark. Our party was formed into different groups, each having a large fire of its own, without which, from the coldness of the nights at this season of the year, it would be impossible to sleep in comfort. These different fires had, from the background where I was, a very beautiful effect, and enabled me to observe the scene before me. Some were busily employed cooking; others were smoking, making their huts, or cutting down timber for fuel, and reminded me by their various occupations of what I had read of a camp of gipsies or the bivouacs of a continental army. I remained here a short time, and then retired to rest for the night in my hammock, swung between two poles, and covered with a tarpaulin, by the side of a comfortable fire large enough to roast an ox.

Thursday, April 27.

After sleeping tolerably well, I rose at daylight, and began to get part of the baggage off, which, however, could not be effected before nine o'clock, as the bullocks and horses were to be collected and fed and their drivers to breakfast before they started; the remainder of the baggage was got off about an hour later. Before we left the ground, the Governor and Mrs. Macquarie and a few more walked down to the spring where we had been supplied with water, situated about a mile down a deep glen. In rainy seasons the water might be had much nearer, as there appears a watercourse at the back of the encampment, which extends down to the spring issuing from a rock. The water is good, but something of a mineral quality. From this spring and the surrounding forest, the Governor gave the name of Spring Wood to this station. We did not leave this place till twelve o'clock, the day cool and pleasant. Our road was stony, and some very severe and short hills for the loaded carts. About five miles further on we came to a very extensive prospect from a lofty spot, where we found a heap of stones, supposed to have been placed there by an adventurer, who had penetrated thus far with much difficulty in his endeavour to cross the mountains. He had arrived at it from a different direction from the one we had now taken, and much more difficult, but finding this place no end to the mountains, and the country looking most unpromising around him, and his provisions being nearly expended, he gave up what he thought a fruitless attempt, and retraced his steps, after erecting this pile of stones, to which the Governor gave the name of Keely's [Caley's] Repulse. About half a mile on we prepared a bridge extending from one rock to another across a chasm, which we named Bluff Bridge, and eight and a half miles further brought us to another grand and extensive view of the country we had left for many miles, from a flat elevated land, which we named the King's Tableland. Two miles more brought us to our resting place for the night, making the whole distance sixteen miles. We came late to our ground, and some of the carts were not up till long after dark. At this place is situated the second depot; twenty-eight miles from the ford was made another station for provisions for the working parties on the road. A good store has been built here, in which we dined. Very little feeding for the cattle at this place; only a kind of coarse grass such as generally grows in swamps, but plenty of excellent water. Found this station a very cold one; during the night the wind blew across the swamp in our rear, which made the night uncomfortable, and obliged me to get up frequently to mend our fires.

Friday, April 28.
Rose before daylight; the morning very cold and threatened rain; but as the sun rose, the clouds and fog cleared away, and we had a fine morning; breakfasted before we moved and sent off the baggage. About four and a half miles on our road this morning, we emerged on a sudden from a most dreary waste to a small rising ground on our left, where one of the grandest views that can be imagined was opened to our sight. In the foreground was a deep glen, part of which we had seen yesterday, and around it an immense amphitheatre of lofty hills crowned with rocks, upon which the sun was shining affording a variety of tints. In the distance were lofty mountains as far as the eye could reach, forming a grand circumference, and background—the whole coup d'oeil grand beyond the power of my pen to describe; and until now most likely unseen by the eye of civilised man. Called it Pitt's Amphitheatre … A little before two o'clock came to our resting-place, forty-one miles from Emu Plains and thirteen from our last ground … Altered the plan of my bed, and made a small tent of the tarpaulin, and slept better than I had done since I had been out.

Saturday, April 29.
About eleven o'clock, at the forty-nine mile tree, we came to the pass down the mountain into the new country below, which could be seen to great advantage from the projecting rock on the left just before descending the pass, and forms a very beautiful and pleasant contrast to the one we had been

travelling over, appearing to be an open forest land with fine
grazing. This pass had been made with great labour down a
very steep mountain of upwards of six hundred feet, and the
way the road is made traversing the face of it makes it nearly
a mile long; it was with much difficulty and exertion we got
the carts down by fixing drag-ropes behind and holding on
with the people; it was so perpendicular in places that the
cattle could scarcely keep their footing. We, however, in about
two hours' hard work, got them all down in safety, and after
allowing the cattle to rest for half a hour at the foot of the
pass, we moved on five miles further through a plain open
forest land to our station on the banks of a small stream, which
the Governor called Cox's River. The pass was likewise named
Cox's Pass, in compliment to the gentleman who had super-
intended making the road and pass—a piece of work which
certainly reflects great credit on his exertions and perseverance. The hill itself was called Mount York, a deep and
extensive glen to the left extending several miles to Prince
Regent's Glen, and the valley which we rode through to Cox's
River the Vale of Clwydd, through its resemblance to a place
of that name in Wales. At the river where we encamped was
plenty of excellent grazing with abundance of water running
over a rocky bed of black granite with a bridge thrown over
it. We arrived at this station a little after three o'clock, a good
deal fatigued with our day's work ...

Thursday, May 4.
Rose this morning just as the day began to dawn. After dressing took a walk along the rising ground behind the camp to
contemplate the beauties of the surrounding country, and
hail the rising sun. The fog continued in the valley I had
quitted, and here and there a hill was seen peeping through
it, appearing like so many islands and a long line of coast
forming a deep and beautiful bay, the fog having the resemblance of water. This day was to be our last march to arrive at
the grand depot and Bathurst Plains ... The Governor and
his party overtook me on the road, and a little after, about
seven miles, we descended the hills, to an extensive plain,

which, in honour of the Minister for the Colonies, was called
Bathurst Plains, being the most extensive of any we had yet
seen, of many miles in length, with the Macquarie running
through it, upon the banks of which the Grand Depot is
situated. Mr. Evans, the Deputy Assistant Surveyor-General,
met us as soon as we descended into the plain. He had been
sent over from Van Diemen's Land to attend the Governor, as
he had already explored this part of the country, and had
been sent forward a second time to make further discoveries,
and was now returned but a day or two to Bathurst before
our arrival, and reported that he had endeavoured to trace
the river, but found that it was not navigable for any distance.
He had met with a very broken and fine grazing country to
the south-west for fifty miles, and fit for every purpose of
cultivation.

On our approach within half a mile of the settlement,
the Governor and Mrs. Macquarie got out of their carriage,
and mounted their saddle horses, and the remainder of the
party, which had straggled behind, coming up, we drew up
into line, twelve in number, and advanced in this order towards the huts, situated on a little rising ground on the banks
of the river. We were received by the party stationed here
with presented arms and three cheers, and, to add to our
satisfaction, we discovered several of the natives of this new
country among them, who were made spectators of the novel
sight.

At first they appeared very much astonished at us, and
not a little alarmed at our reception, but in a short time by
kind treatment, they became more reconciled to us, and
seemed to cast off all fear. Our people received strict injunc-
tions to treat them kindly, to put no restraints upon their
movements, but to let them come and go when they thought
proper. They had nothing with them but a couple of rude
spears which they threw down near one of the huts, and
seemed perfectly careless about them. One old man was blind
of an eye, which the people stationed here said was frequently
the case both with the men and women; but this man and an
old woman we one day met in the woods were the only

instances we saw of the kind during our stay. They resembled the natives about Sydney, but did not speak the same language; they appeared, however, to be one degree more advanced towards civilisation than our old friends, possessing some art in manufacturing themselves cloaks of skins, very neatly sewed together by the sinews of the kangaroo and emu, and carved on the inside with a variety of figures. These cloaks were for the sole purpose of keeping themselves warm, and not out of any regard for decency, for in the middle of the day, when the weather was warm, they threw them carelessly over their shoulders. What little I saw of them during our stay, they appeared to be a harmless and inoffensive race, with nothing forbidding or ferocious in their countenances. On the contrary, they are perfectly mild and cheerful, and laugh at everything they see and repeat everything they hear. As I had sent on a man the day before to pitch one of the tents for the Governor, we found it ready for us, but we preferred dining in the store, which was very neatly made and well thatched.

Friday, May 5.
After breakfast was over, the Governor and the rest of the party set off to visit some of the country on the other side of the river, crossing at a ford a little below the huts. I remained at home to see the tents pitched and the things put in order, as we proposed staying here a week; employed at this the whole of the day till dinner-time. The spot which was chosen for the Governor's large tent was upon a little rising ground about three hundred yards from the men's huts; a small tent was placed on each side with a clear space in front upon which a small flagstaff was erected. This was a delightful spot for a town, commanding a view of the surrounding country for a considerable extent; the soil excellent, fitted for every purpose of cultivation, with abundance of good water near at hand, but the wood is scarce, being obliged to send upwards of a mile for it. A native dog was killed as I was pitching the tents, by our dogs. These animals fight very fiercely; the natives domesticate them, and make use of them in hunting

their game, the kangaroo and the emu, and in their tame state (when accompanied by their masters) often get the better of our dogs. They very much resemble the fox, and seem to be a breed between that and the wolf; but as none of these animals are found in the country, it is difficult to say how these dogs have become inmates of it.

Saturday, May 6.
After breakfast this morning, mounted our horses and rode through the country for a few miles to the northward to a small stream running through a pretty little valley, which we called Winburndale, giving the creek the same name. The ground we rode over was good, both for grazing and cultivation, plentifully watered, and very thinly wooded; gave chase to some kangaroos, and killed a small one with the dogs; the ground bad to gallop over, being full of holes and tufts of grass. Yesterday a black swan was shot and brought into the camp, weighing ten pounds; it was the largest one of the kind I had ever seen, measuring six feet two inches from the tip of each wing, and was four feet three inches long, including the neck, which was two feet ... there was another with him at the time he was shot, which was afterwards seen flying over the camp, and I heard him again crying for his mate. They seem to show great feeling, and seldom live long after losing their companions. A gentleman at Sydney had a couple of these birds. One of them died, and being skinned by his servants, the skin was put in the garden to dry; the other found out the remains of his companion, and laid down beside it, where it remained without moving, refusing all sustenance, and in a day or two was found dead stretched out on the skin.

We had another visit from the natives this day, who came in with the utmost confidence, and slept in the camp, getting as close to the fire as they could without burning. The nights were very cold, and the mornings foggy, and they seemed to feel the cold very acutely. They came into the tents while we were dressing, without any ceremony, but seemed, after the first surprise at the novelty of the surrounding objects, to be totally devoid of curiosity. They took everything that was offered to them, but asked for nothing. If you put a question to them, or held anything to find out its name in their language, they only repeated the words you made use of, following, however, very accurately the sound. One word they soon learned and seemed to understand, 'Good-bye,' which they repeated at night when they quitted the tents.

Sunday, May 7
A thick foggy morning, which soon cleared away as the sun got a little power. A little after breakfast, assembled the whole of our inhabitants, civic, naval and military, seventy-five in number, and drawing them up in line, in front of the large tent, the British flag was displayed for the first time in this new country, the troops saluting it with three volleys, and the rest giving three cheers. The Governor then delivered a short speech to Mr. Cox and Mr. Evans as having through their exertions been brought to so fine a country, thanking the latter for having explored it with so much perseverance and success, and the former for having with considerable labour made so good a road for upwards of a hundred miles in so short a time and so difficult to perform. He then named the place and new town to be marked out, 'Bathurst', and each drank a bumper, some in wine and the rest in rum, to the King's health, and success to the town of Bathurst—an era in my life, which at some future day I hope I shall look back to with pleasure and satisfaction. We then adjourned to the Governor's marquee, where Divine service was performed, a suitable ceremony at the close of so interesting a one we had just been witness to. 'Tis pleasing to look forward and think that perhaps at some future period not far distant, a flourishing town may arise on the very spot we are now occupying on the banks of the Macquarie River, which may hand down the name of our worthy Governor with honour to posterity, as its founder; and where Divine service has now been performed to the great Dispenser of events, some future church may be erected to His name and worship. The men were orderly and attentive and the day was spent with

cheerfulness, and good humour, and was closed by giving the men another dram ...

Wednesday, May 10.
A very thick foggy morning, which did not clear away till late. We made this a resting day for our horses, and I took a walk up the river about four miles to try for some fish. Could not get a bite; crossed over the river and returned to the camp, where I found some of the natives who had arrived during my absence, and shortly after my return some more came in. There were three men, and a number of fine lads, but no women, nor had we seen one since our arrival, except the old lady we met in the woods. They submitted very quietly to have their hair cut, and we clothed them with some shirts and jackets and trousers, and gave to each a leather cap, and a tommyhawk; the latter present appeared to please them most. To one of the best-looking men of the party the Governor gave a piece of yellow cloth in exchange for his skin cloak. They stayed with us the whole of the day, and left us in the evening to return to their encampment over the hills, but did not seem to wish us to follow them, which we did not attempt to do.

Thursday, May 11.
This morning was likewise very foggy, which the sun had not power to clear away till nearly ten o'clock. This being the day we were to commence our journey back, sent off some of the carts at nine o'clock. And after breakfast, when most of the baggage was ready, and the saddle-horses standing around the carts, those men who it was intended should remain behind, were assembled before the Governor when he exhorted them to conduct themselves peaceably towards the natives, to treat them kindly whenever they met with them, and endeavour to keep the friendly intercourse which then subsisted; which the men promised to do and in testimony of their thanks for the kind treatment they had received, and their acquiescence in the order, they gave three cheers, when immediately, as with one consent, away started

all the carts, and some of the saddle horses, going off in different ways full gallop. In a moment all was confusion and dismay, expecting every instant to see the carts overturned and everything in them dashed to pieces. Fortunately however, they were all stopped without sustaining much damage. Two caravans belonging to the gentlemen were upset, and the shaft on one broken. We soon collected our scattered forces together, and moved off, bidding adieu to Bathurst, and its inhabitants, not without a feeling of regret and sincere wishes that the town we had established might flourish and become a thriving settlement.

We marched ten miles, and arrived at our former station at the Campbell River, in two hours and encamped on the same spot. We found this day one of the warmest we had experienced. Our road was very good, mostly on the descent. On our arrival at our ground we found most of the grass burned up, owing, I suppose, to the fires we had left behind us. It had not, fortunately, spread to any distance, and we found quite enough for our horses. One emu was killed yesterday and we had some of it cooked for breakfast this morning. It was very good eating, tasting like beef, a little dry and tough; it weighed eighty-six pounds, and was a very large bird.

Friday, May 12.
Got up this morning an hour before day; could not sleep, the night very cold. After breakfast moved off, and at twelve arrived at Sidmouth Valley, halted there for about an hour to give the horses a mouthful of grass and a little water, and then moved on seven miles further to the Fish River, and encamped near our old station; distance twenty miles. On mustering our followers yesterday we found one man missing. He had come with us with the idea of becoming a settler in the new country, and as we suppose, he had remained behind at Bathurst, a man was this morning sent back for him, he returned in the evening and reported the last time the poor fellow was seen was with some of the natives. He had been at Bathurst the morning we left, and being a little

in liquor, had insisted upon going with them to their camp, where it was supposed from his own imprudence he had fallen a sacrifice, as no trace could be found of him by the parties which had been sent out; and the natives with whom he had gone away had not since been seen. I am told he has left a wife and four children to lament his loss, which likewise threw a damp upon all our spirits, and considerably diminished the pleasure of our journey back ...

Monday, May 15.
Rose early this morning, and sent off what remained of the baggage to the pass, intending to breakfast there before we ascended. Arrived there at nine o'clock, found most of the carts had got up safe, but with much labour and difficulty. During our breakfast the carriage was taken up and by twelve o'clock we were all safe at the top without any accident whatever, which was more than I expected. After arriving at the top, I walked on for a few miles, when a very thick fog came on, which at first I took for the smoke of a large fire in the woods, it continued so for the remainder of the day, and obliged us to dine in the tent. Our march this day was six miles, to the foot of the pass; one up and eight more to our ground. The fog continued the whole of the night, and the weather was much milder than we had found it for some nights past. From the appearance of this station, it being a kind of a heath, but a very wild and dreary scenery, the Governor gave it the name of Blackheath, though to my eye, very unlike its namesake.

Tuesday, May 16.
Breakfasted early, and got all the baggage off before nine, the morning was foggy, but the sun soon cleared it away, and having a tolerably good ride this day, we got to our ground at the second depot by one o'clock. The Governor changed the name of this station to Jamison's Valley, in compliment to Sir John Jamison, who was one of our party. The night proved very cold, the wind blowing from the same quarter as it did when we were last here, but with greater violence.

Wednesday, May 17.

… I partook of a good dinner and went to bed early. As this was the last night of our being together, served out an extra allowance of grog to the men, and had some very good songs from them, and all around us appeared contented and happy.

Thursday, May 18.

Rose this morning at the usual hour of daylight, and having breakfasted, started from our ground at Spring Wood at ten o'clock, our road was descent the whole of the way to the ford, twelve miles, where we arrived in two hours, and after crossing the Nepean, our party began to separate, Sir John Jamison, Mr. Oxley, and Mr. Cox going to their farms, and Mr. Campbell to follow us to Sydney. The rest of the party went on with us to Mrs. King's farm, where we were met by Mr. Hassall, who provided a dinner for us on our return. In thus taking leave of the friends who had accompanied us on our expedition, I cannot help mentioning with satisfaction, the unanimity and good understanding which subsisted between every individual composing our small society. Not a word of ill-humour passed the whole time; on the contrary everyone appeared to use his endeavour to make the time pass as pleasantly as possible. As I was resolved not to indulge in the luxury of a bed till I arrived home, I wrapped myself up in my boat cloak, and notwithstanding the hardness of the boards, slept very well till morning.

Friday, May 19.

As this was to be our last stage, set off at seven o'clock from Mrs. King's farm in company with Mr. Hassall, and after a pleasant ride of sixteen miles, arrived at Parramatta, where we breakfasted, and resting our horses till eleven o'clock, returned to Sydney, after an absence of twenty-four days. We had the happiness to find all well at home, and I hope were grateful for the protection which had been afforded us on our journey, no accidents having occurred the whole of the way but the loss of a few horses, and the loss of the poor fellow at Bathurst.

IV

Elizabeth Hawkins

A party of females

G overnor Macquarie was ambivalent about opening
up the land to the west. Like some of the governors
before him, he was more interested in controlling
the convicts while they were in captivity, and turning them
into small crop farmers once they became free, than in the
interests of wealthy free settlers who wanted large spreads on
which to run sheep and cattle. He was also concerned about
conflict with Aborigines. After the road was built, soldiers
were stationed on it and anyone wishing to cross the mountains was supposed to apply for a pass.

Cox had already driven some of his own cattle over
while building the road, and government cattle were taken
over soon after it opened. Lawson took up his land grant and
in 1819 was appointed Commandant of Bathurst, which became a government settlement. In 1822 Thomas Hawkins,
newly arrived in the colony, was appointed commissariat storekeeper at Bathurst. He crossed the mountains with his wife,
Elizabeth, his seventy-year-old mother-in-law, and his eight
children, whose ages ranged from one to twelve. Apparently
this was the first family of white free settlers to make the
crossing. This is the account of the journey that Elizabeth

sent to her sister in London. As she explains, it was written in less than ideal circumstances, which no doubt accounts for its few confusing sentences.

My dear Ann,

I told you in my last of our intended journey across the Blue Mountains; we have accomplished it, and as I think it may prove interesting to you I shall be very particular in my account of it. It took some time after my last to make the necessary arrangements here for a house to receive us, and for us to be certain of the necessary assistance from the Governor before we could leave Sydney; all was ready on 4th April (Good Friday), and on the morning of the 5th we commenced our journey. We had many presents and kind wishes from those around us, indeed there was not a dry eye in the family of our landlord.

You, or no one in England, will hardly credit me when I tell you the number of horses, bullocks, carts etc., requisite to convey us, when we possessed no furniture but one table and twelve chairs; these, with our cooking utensils, bedding and a few agricultural implements, groceries and other necessaries to last us a few months, with our clothes, constituted the whole of our luggage. We had a wagon with six bullocks, a dray with five, another dray with three horses, a cart with two, and, last of all, a tilted cart, with mother, myself, and seven children, with two horses. Hawkins and Tom rode on horseback. The cavalcade moved slowly on, the morning was fine, and the road equal to any turnpike road in England, with a forest on each side; but the sun is not prevented from reaching the earth, as all the trees are lofty and only branch from the top. When within a few miles of Parramatta, Hawkins rode on to the factory for a female servant who had been selected for us. He rejoined us whilst we were partaking our dinner at the foot of a tree. We arrived rather late in the evening at Rooty Hill, a distance of twenty-five miles; the government house was ready to receive us.

The next day being Sunday, we rested, partly to recover from the fatigue we had previous to leaving Sydney,
and because the general orders were, there should be no travelling on Sunday. I could have been contented to have
remained there for ever—the house was good and the land
all around like a fine wooded park in England.

On Monday we resumed our journey, and for nine
miles found the road the same as before. We had now reached
the Nepean River, which you cross to Emu Plains, where
there is a government house and depot, but beyond these
there are no habitations until you reach Bathurst, excepting a
solitary house at the different places where people sleep. We
had to wait at a hut many times [hours] until horses and carts
were ready on the opposite side, as those which brought us
from Sydney were to leave. We could only get part of our
luggage over that night, and Sir John Jamison, who resided
near, sent his head constable to guard the rest during the
night. The next day it rained hard, but through fear it might
continue, when the water rushing from the mountains makes
all the rivers in this country dangerous and impassable, we
had the rest of our things brought over.

The next day was occupied in getting things dry, and
the following one in making necessary preparations for the
journey, unpacking many things to ensure their greater safety,
arranging our provisions and bedding to enable us to get at
them more conveniently. This being done at five o'clock,
Hawkins and I went to dine with Sir J. Jamison, who had
invited a lady and two gentlemen to meet us; here we partook of a sumptuous repast, consisting of mock-turtle soup,
boiled fowls, round of beef, delicious fish of three kinds, cur-
ried duck, goose and wild-fowl, Madeira and Burgundy, with
various liquors and English ale. I mention all this to show
you his hospitality, and convince you it is possible for people
to live here as well as in England.

I was delighted with his garden. The apples and quinces
were larger than I ever saw them before (it is now autumn in
this country), and many early trees of the former were again
in blossom. The vines had a second crop of grapes, and the

fig trees a third crop. The peaches and apricots here are standing trees. He has English cherries, plums and filberts [type of
hazelnut]. These, with oranges, lemons, limes and citrons,
medlars [tree of the rose family, with fruit like brown-skinned
apples], almonds, rock and water melons, with all the common fruits of England; vegetables of all kinds and grown at
all seasons of the year, which shows how fine the climate is.

The next morning, Friday, the 12th, we re-loaded.
Sir John came to see us off, and presented us with a quarter
of mutton, a couple of fowls, and some butter. I had now
before me this tremendous journey. I was told I deserved to
be immortalised for the attempt, and that Government could
not do too much for us for taking such a family to a settlement where none had ever gone before—I mean no family
of free settlers, and very few others. Everything that could be
done for us was done by the officers to make it as comfortable as possible.

In addition to our luggage, we had to take corn for
the cattle, as in the mountains there is not sufficient grass for
them, and we also had provisions for ourselves and the nine
men that accompanied us. In consequence of this we were
obliged to leave many things behind. We now commenced
with two drays, with five bullocks each; one dray with four
horses, and our own cart with two; they had no more carts to
give us. Amidst the good wishes of all, not excepting a party
of natives who had come to bid us welcome, we commenced
our journey. We had not proceeded more than a quarter of a
mile before we came to a small stream of water, with a sandy
bottom and banks; here the second dray with the bullocks
sank. The storekeeper, superintendent, and overseer from
Emu, witnessing our stoppage, came to our assistance; the
two latter did not quit us until night. It employed us an hour
to extricate the dray, and it was not accomplished without
the horses of the other being added to it. We now slowly
proceeded about a quarter of a mile further and now, my
dear, imagine me at the foot of a tremendous mountain, the
difficulty of passing which is, I suppose, as great or greater
than any known road in the world, not for the road being

bad, as it has been made, and is hard all the way, but the difficulty lies in the extreme steepness of the ascent and descent, the hollow places, and the large rugged pieces of rock. You will, perhaps, imagine, as I had done, that the mountains are perfectly barren. For forty miles they are barren of herbage for cattle, but as far as the eye can reach, even from the summit of the highest, every hill and dale is covered with wood, lofty trees, and small shrubs, many of them blooming with the most delicate flowers, the colours so beautiful that the highest circles in England would prize them. These mountains appear solid rock, hardly any earth on the surface; this land seems as if it were never intended for human beings to inhabit. There are no roots or substitutes for bread; no fruits or vegetables on which men could subsist, but almost everything will grow which is brought to it.

We now began our ascent up the first Lapstone Hill, so called from all the stones being like a cobbler's lapstone. The horses got on very well, but the bullocks could not, so we were obliged to unload, have a cart from Emu and send back some of the luggage. Even then the horses were obliged, when they reached the top, to return and assist them. We only performed the distance of one mile and a half that day. Our tent was for the first time pitched. The fatigue to mother and myself was very great every night after the journey in preparing beds and giving the children their food. The little ones were generally tired and cross; little Edward in particular.

It was a lovely moonlight night, and all was novelty and delight to the elder children. Immense fires were made in all directions. We gave them their supper, and after putting the younger ones to bed, I came from the tent, in front of which was a large fire, our drays and carts close in view. The men—nine in number—were busily employed in cooking in one place, our own man roasting a couple of fowls for our next day's journey; at another the men [convicts], not the most prepossessing in their appearance, with the glare of the fires and the reflection of the moon shining on them, in the midst of a forest, formed altogether such a scene as I cannot describe. It resembled more a party of banditti, such as I have read of, than anything else. I turned from the view, took the arm of Hawkins, who was seated at the table with the store-keeper, and went to the back of the tent. Here we saw Tom and the three eldest girls trying who could make the best fire, as happy as it was possible for young hearts to be. Then I seemed to pause. It was a moment I shall never forget. For the first time for many a long month I seemed capable of enjoying and feeling the present moment without a dread for the future. 'Tis true we had in a manner bade adieu to the world, to our country and our friends, but in our country we could no longer provide for our children, and the world from that cause had lost all its charm. You, Bowling, and all my friends and acquaintances, I thought of with regret, but the dawn of independence was opening on us. Hawkins was again an officer under Government, a home to receive us, and the certainty under any circumstances of never wanting the common necessaries of life. You, my dear Ann, must have suffered in mind what we had long suffered, to form an idea of what we then felt. After a little while we returned to the table. These were moments of such inward rest that Hawkins took up a flute belonging to one of the party, and calling Eliza to us, she danced in a place where perhaps no one of her age had ever trod before.

The next morning we took our breakfast, and packing up our beds and provisions, prepared to depart, but during the night our team of bullocks and Hawkins' horse had returned to Emu. It was thought most desirable that we, with two drays, and Tom for our guard, should proceed to Springwood, as there was a house to go into. From the difficulty they had the preceding day with the bullocks they took from our cart the two horses, and gave us two bullocks. After a most fatiguing journey of nine miles we arrived. The house was inhabited by a corporal and two soldiers, kept there, I believe, to superintend the Government stock. Formerly a greater number of men were kept there, and there was a large room or store where provisions had been kept. A good barn in England would have been a palace to this place. There was a large kitchen, with an immense fireplace, and two small rooms behind. With the exception of a green in front, the house was completely in the wood.

The corporal's wife, an old woman, who had been transported above twenty years, with fawning manner, came forward to show us in. We entered the kitchen, which contained a long table and form, and some stumps of trees to answer the purpose of chairs, of which there was not one in the house. Several people were here to rest for the night, journeying from Bathurst to Sydney. We were shown into the small back room, which had nothing in it but a sofa, with slips of bark laid on it for the seat. Here I felt desolate and lonely. It was nearly dark; still Hawkins did not arrive, and we got quite miserable. At length the storekeeper from Emu arrived, and said to us that he could not get on without some horses being sent to his assistance. It was nearly nine o'clock before he arrived. I went out (it was dark), but such a scene of confusion as there appeared from the glare of the fires, the carts and drays, the men, tired with their day's work, swearing as they extricated the bullocks and horses. It was long before I could distinguish Hawkins. I felt comparatively safe when I did. The old woman, a most depraved character and well-known thief, with a candle held high above her head, screamed out, 'Welcome to Springwood, sir!'

He said, when he looked round, he felt sure his welcome would be the loss of whatever she could steal from us. He was much fatigued, not having had any refreshment all day. It was my intention when I first arrived to have pitched one tent on the green, but it unfortunately was on top of the dray left with Hawkins, but having my mattresses, I spread them in the storeroom. The earth was dirty, damp and cold. We could not think of undressing the children, and when in bed all looked most miserable. I lay down with my baby. A very few minutes convinced me I should get no rest. The bugs were crawling by hundreds. The children were restless with them and the confinement of their clothes. The old woman had contrived to steal some spirits from our provision basket, which with what had been given to her made her and the soldiers tipsy. All was noise and confusion indoors; without, swearing and wrangling with the men. Never did I pass a night equal to it. Hawkins remained all night on the green or in the cart watching. In addition to other noises, a flock of sheep had been driven into the yard, and they, to avoid the men, came close to the house and kept up a continual pat with their feet. Could any of our romance writers have been in my situation they might have planned an interesting scene to add to the horrors of their volumes. You may be certain we were happy when the morning came. We got our breakfast, and packing up our beds, bade adieu to the house at Springwood.

Mother, myself, and three girls, as the morning was fair, walked on before. It was such a relief to get away from that place that I never enjoyed a walk more. We gathered most delicate nosegays from the flowering shrubs that grew amongst the trees. You must understand that the whole of the road from beginning to the end of the mountains is cut entirely through a forest, nor can you go in a direct line to Bathurst from one mountain to another, but you are obliged often to wind round the edges of them, and at times to look down such precipices as would make you shudder. We ascended. Our cart had now three bullocks, as we had so much trouble to get on with two, but we were worse off than ever. As the ascent became worse they refused to drag, and every few minutes first one and then another would lie down. The dogs were summoned to bark at them and bite their noses to make them get up. The barking of the dogs, the bellowing of the bullocks and the swearing of the men made our heads ache, and kept us in continual terror. That was exactly the case every day of the journey. Frequently it was necessary we should all get out, and more frequently our fears made us scream out: 'Oh, do let us get out. I am sure there is danger.' At length we came to a hill so steep it seemed as if we could never get up it. We alighted, and seating ourselves on a fallen tree, waited for the event. We were on the side of it; in front it was almost perpendicular; behind was a valley so deep the eye could hardly distinguish the trees at the bottom. To gain the top of this mountain the road wound along the side. The first dray with the horses got up. They were then brought back to assist the rest with the bullocks, but they could not succeed in raising them from one rock to another. With great noise a sudden effort was made, and one shaft was broken. This had to be repaired as well as we could, some of the luggage was taken off, and with the assistance of the other horses, etc., it was got up; the other was got up in like manner. When at the top the men, who were much fatigued, sought for a spring of water, and with the addition of a bottle of rum, were refreshed. We again set off, and for the last two miles it was perfectly dark, attended by heavy rain. You can suppose the danger and misery we rode in, not being able to see where we went. We were obliged to go on until we came to water. There our tent was pitched in the road, and was dark, damp, and dirty. We were obliged to remain in the cart until the bedding was put in the tent. Of course we again lay down in our clothes. This very fatiguing day's journey we had only accomplished eight miles. For fear I should tire you with a repetition of the same scenes, I will now tell you that every day on the journey from Emu to Bathurst we were subject to the same things, such as our bullocks lying down constantly; the others, not able to draw their load, compelled to have the assistance of the horses, which caused great delay.

Our provisions consisted of half a pig, which was salted for us at Emu, and some beef. We had flour to make bread, tea, sugar, butter, and when we stopped at night we made our tea and had some cold meat. It was our man's business every night to boil a piece of meat for the next day, and bake a cake under the iron pot. Breakfast and supper were the only meals we had. I used to take a small basket in the cart with me, a little just to keep us from starving, and some drink for baby, and during the eleven nights we rested in the woods, Hawkins never laid down until about three in the morning, when the overseer would get up and watch, and never but twice did he take his clothes off; as we occupied the tent, his only resting place was the cart. It rained the next morning, and everything was very uncomfortable. The men went in

search of the cattle (they were obliged to be turned loose at
night to get water and food), could not find them at all. After
waiting some time, we thought it better to proceed, excepting one dray, which the overseer was to watch while his men
sought the bullocks. As the road this day was something better, we got nine miles to two bark huts, which had been
erected by the men employed in mending the roads, but were
now empty. We were very glad to take possession of one, and
our men of the other, as it rained all day.

In England you never saw anything like these huts,
and I fear from my description you will not understand them.
Some stakes of trees are stuck in the ground, the outside bark
from the trees is tied together, and to these with narrow strips
of what is called stringy bark; being tough, it answers the
purpose of cord, and the roof is done in the same manner.
There was a kind of chimney but neither window nor door,
but a space left to enter. As many men had been obliged to
sleep here, all round were placed small stakes, and across and
on the top were laid pieces of bark, so as to form a kind of
broad shelf all round. Here we spread our beds. Mother and
I soon found it was impossible to get any rest from the bugs
and fleas. Helen and Louisa were laid head and foot. Finding
them restless, we looked, and found, poor things, that from
some of the pieces of bark not being close to the outside,
they had tumbled through, and being suspended by their arms,
we had some difficulty to drag them up.

The next morning another overseer came to us from
Emu to say the bullocks had again reached home, but would
be sent to the dray with two more to assist us. We were obliged
to wait that day at the huts for its arrival, and now Mr. Riley,
a person who had acted as assistant to the former storekeeper
at Bathurst, and who had left Emu with us [found that] two
young horses belonging to Government, which he was to
take to Bathurst, [had] got away from him, and could not be
found. He had likewise lost his bridle, but declared he would
hasten on and get the commandant to send us some assistance. With a piece of rope round his horse's face, and slips
of sheepskin tied to it for a bridle, and a merry heart he left

us. Another night was forced to be passed in the hut without rest. The next morning was fine, and we again ascended the cart. This day we accomplished nine miles, much in the same way as before. The following morning, the 18th, a morning never to be forgotten, for to all my complaints about the road I was continually silenced by, 'Say nothing about it until you get to the big hill.' We were now within eleven miles of it, but the road being tolerably good and the morning fine, in expectation of something very wonderful, our spirits were by no means bad, for after this day our greatest difficulties were over. Hawkins shot some birds, the boys hunted a kangaroo rat; we laughed and talked, and went cheerfully on until we were within a mile of Mount York, or more commonly called the 'Big Hill'. I desired Tom to ride on and give us some account of it. He soon came galloping back. 'Oh! Ma, you will never get up, I am sure you won't. [Presumably Tom said, or meant to say, *down*.] I can't see much of the road, but I can see the valley you are to reach. It is dreadful.' Our courage began to fail by the time we reached the top.

Here, my dear Ann, I think I had better stop. I leave it to your imagination. I feel it out of my power to give a proper description of it. I have offered the pen to Hawkins, but he refuses. I tell him I must take a leap from top to bottom, but that he will not allow, so I must write on as well as I can. So now all stopped to recover resolution. I gave all something to eat and some wine to drink. The men began to cut down trees necessary to chain behind the drays. This appeared a terrible precaution to take. We thought it better to commence our walk down. First Tom led his pony, Hawkins his horse. We had proceeded but a short distance when it appeared so impossible for any cart to descend the place we were at that Hawkins refused to go any further with me. Ann was forced to be carried, and mother and myself had to carry Edward. How we got down I cannot tell, but I believe the fear lest any accident should happen to him gave us strength and resolution to keep our own footing. We were often obliged to sit down on a fallen tree, but when we did the pains in our legs and the violent trembling all over us made it difficult to get up again. We at last reached the bottom in safety.

To give an account of the road is not in my power, but you have read Miss Porter's *Scottish Chiefs*, where the rocks and glens are so well described; but even that can convey but a faint idea of this mountain. The descent is about a mile. It is four thousand feet above the level of the sea, all rocks and cavities, awfully grand to behold, but from it being impossible to make some parts of the road safe from the projecting pieces of rock, we were rendered very uneasy about our luggage. It was about three o'clock when we seated ourselves on some trees. It was extremely hot. I had given a piece of sugar candy to one of the children in a small tin can we had brought down, and as Tom and Eliza found a spring of water, the can became useful to us to drink from and the sugar served to quiet the little ones. We waited a considerable time, could hear nothing of the rest, and then desired Tom to go and meet them, and when he found them safe, to call out. An hour passed and still we heard nothing. Mother and I then thought to walk a little way and listen. Sometimes we could just hear the sound of voices, and all again was still. We returned to our children. It was nearly sunset, and in this country it is dark almost immediately. I asked Eliza if she would venture up with the female servant to inquire what we were to do, as I was convinced some accident had happened. It was nearly dark when they returned with two cloaks, lantern, and tinder-box, on account of the first dray having upset at what is called the 'Forty-nine mile pinch,' and [saying] that the cart would be sent down to us. I soon after heard Tom's voice high above my head. I blamed him for keeping me so long in suspense, but he said I had desired him to call if they were safe, which he did as soon as the dray was unloaded and reloaded. Tired as we were, all were employed in breaking wood and making fires.

It was quite dark before the cart came. In it were two great coats and a shawl, a piece of bread, and a little arrowroot. I gave it to the poor children. To little Neddy I gave the arrowroot, and we hushed him off to sleep. Mother sat down with him in her lap before a fire. Ann and George were wrapped up and laid on the ground beside her. The four girls I laid in the cart with a great coat over them. I began to feel very weary and chilly. About nine, two drays arrived, but to stand and listen as I had previously done to the noise of the men endeavouring to cheer the cattle, and the dreadful rumbling with which they descended, was enough to create a sensation of terror in a very stout heart; to see them was impossible until they got close to us. Hawkins was still at the top of the hill, remaining with the last drays, which from the darkness and the fatigue of the horses and men it was found could not be got down that night. They had now to get water and put the tea-kettle on, and some were obliged to walk up the hill and bring down our provisions, and many things which we could not do without, and two men to remain and watch the dray. Hawkins came down with the others, very much fatigued. We now had our supper and the tent pitched. It was eleven o'clock when ready for us. We got the children from the ground and cart into it, and laid ourselves down.

The next morning we all felt the effects of being exposed so long to the night air, and the great fatigue we had. After breakfast we walked up to a small rock, and, sitting down, viewed the scene around, and felt thankful that the little property we possessed was safe, for the injury caused by the dray's upsetting was trifling. Here as we sat we observed three persons winding among the trees in the valley on horseback. They proved to be a clergyman from Parramatta, another gentleman, and a servant. They spoke in rapture of the country from which they were returning.

I now felt myself so ill from fatigue that I was forced to go into the tent and lie down. I fell asleep, and did not wake until the last dray came rumbling by me. Before commencing the journey again, which we did about one o'clock, I cannot help remarking on the extreme fatigue the men endured the preceding day without any refreshment from breakfast until their supper at eleven o'clock. One man in particular, who was the head driver of our cart, a Folkstone man, a countryman of our own, behaved uncommonly well when the dray overturned. Nothing saved the lives of the horses and our property but the stump of a tree by the road-side. It was suspended over an immense precipice. This man was the first who got on top, and, hanging by the ropes, laboured hard to lighten the dray. He, likewise, was one who went at night to bring down our provisions. Hawkins told him his conduct had been such that he should strongly recommend him to the commanding officer, which he has done, and in all probability he will either be made an overseer of a party, or have a ticket-of-leave given, so that he may work for himself, which is a reward given to them when their behaviour has been very good.

There are but few birds on the mountains, but their plumage is more beautiful than I ever beheld before. They are called 'Blue Mountaineers'. Then, with a green variety of parrots, which may be heard chattering in the trees, there are also birds called 'Laughing Jackasses,' which startled us the preceding evening just at sunset. They appeared to be all round us, making their horrid noise. It was the same at sunrise. I should say there never before was such a party of females without any protection for so many hours at the foot of the mountains. Had any snakes attacked us I fear we should have lost our lives, for none of us would have had the courage to kill them.

Our journey for five miles was very good. We now had reached Cox's River, which has a bridge over it, but a very steep bank to descend, and when there has been much rain on the mountains it is rendered impassable from its over-flowing the bridge. Fortunately we got safe over. We had now reached the spot we had looked forward to from the time of leaving Emu as a place of rest, as here it is customary for all drivers of cattle and luggage to rest for a day or two, as there is good grass. We were all much fatigued. We pitched our tent in a field in front of the house, which was inhabited by a corporal and his wife. She was both clean and civil.

Hearing of our coming, she had procured a bucket of milk, and never was anything more enjoyed.

In the evening, Mr. Lowe, a chief magistrate, arrived, a traveller like ourselves. He commenced his journey in the morning, but we remained. I took this opportunity of giving the children all a good washing and change of clothes. This, as the day was extremely sultry, and not a tree to shade us in the tent, made it, instead of a day of rest, one of great fatigue to me. Being all now so completely sick and tired of the journey, we decided on setting off the next morning, more particularly as the weather was showery and from the season of the year heavy rain might be expected. We were reinforced by a cart and two horses from Bathurst, accompanied by Mr. Riley, as he had promised.

We again ascended our cart on the twenty-first. We had been sitting for some time on the banks of the river seeing the whole cavalcade cross, and when it came to our turn it was with many fears we entered the water nearly up to the horses' bellies, and the bottom covered with large pieces of rock and stone, enough to overturn the cart and jolt us to death. A man offered to carry little Neddie over in his arms. With anxious eyes I watched him through fear his feet might slip and our darling boy have his head dashed against a stone. With talking, swearing, beating our poor bullocks, we got safe on the bank on the opposite side. We had now a very long and steep hill before us, and, as usual, they refused to go. It was decided that we must have two good horses, as it was impossible we could ever get on. 'Sir Noby Redmond' and 'Lion' (names I can never forget) were placed in a dray with a horse behind and another before them, but from it being a constant succession of steep hills, we were only able that day to perform eight miles, and rested at eight in a valley. Here we were joined by five more bullocks from Bathurst.

We set off early next morning; after going eight miles reached the Fish River; after crossing which we had to ascend our last hill, which was very long, very steep. I thought I could never have walked to the top. The drays were a considerable time in getting up, and were obliged to assist each other. We now descended into a most beautiful country to Sidmouth Valley. We had to go through a very bad swamp before we got to our resting place, which was where Mr. Lowe's overseer lived, who had the care of his stock. He had desired his tent to remain for us, and we were very glad to take possession of it, as it was raining here. A gentleman from Bathurst, whom we had known in Sydney, came to meet us, and accompanied us back. We had now, my dear Ann, accomplished our journey over the mountains. The last ten miles we had hardly a spot of level ground; all was steep hills. We were now but eighteen miles from Bathurst, the country extremely beautiful, gently rising hills covered with wood. We passed Macquarie Plains, crossed Fish River, and entered on the plains of Bathurst. The road was good, and, being determined to reach home that night, we almost trotted, which jolted us so dreadfully that I thought every bone would be disjointed. It was as much as we could do to keep ourselves on the seats and hold the children. As if to the very last our journey was to be made uncomfortable, a fine rain began, which beat in our faces, and made us very cold. At length our house was pointed out to us. What a welcome sight! The rain was now powerful, and before we could reach home we had to cross the Macquarie River, the most dangerous of all. You descend a steep bank, and suddenly plunge into the water, which was as high as the bottom of the cart. The first dray got over, but the rest, being lower, we were obliged to seek another ford for them. We remained alone. The driver of the first brought one of his horses over, put it to ours, and in we plunged. We felt more alarmed for our personal safety at that moment than we had done during the whole journey. We reached the opposite side, and all at one moment exclaimed, 'We are over.' A few minutes brought us to our house, where there was a blazing wood fire to warm and cheer us.

I have now, my dear Bowling and Ann, brought you to the end of my journey, but I cannot close this long letter without adding a little more. I tell Hawkins that had it been possible to have gone any further (as he was always famous for moving us about) we should have done it, but beyond here there is no road. Mother bore the fatigue uncommonly well. A journey such as I have described of eighteen days was, at her age, a very great undertaking, but she has recovered from it, and is better than I am, for I am very thin and not very strong. Our children are all well and happy.

On this side of the river the land is chiefly belonging to Government; on the opposite side to the settlers, or, more properly speaking, grants to gentlemen, who as yet have only huts there for the stock-keepers to reside in and they pay only occasional visits.

The Governor is coming in the spring, when great improvements are expected. Two hundred men are to be employed on the roads to make them passable, and a plan for the town will be laid out, and if a chaplain and surgeon are sent we shall have a little society. They are beginning to build a very good brick house for us, which Sir Thomas, on account of our family, has consented shall be of two storeys. It will be some time before it is ready for us, but when we get in we shall be very comfortable. The one we now occupy contains three rooms and a pantry, all brick floors. The front door opens into the sitting room, immediately opposite is the back door, between the two is a ladder which leads into a loft, to which, as yet, there is no trap door. Our bedrooms, likewise, lead from the room, and where we all at present sleep is open to the roof, which is shingled slips of wood, which at a little distance look like slates. Mr. Lawson, the commandant, who resides in the Government House, has ordered two additional rooms to be added, and in another month I hope to be able to sleep in them. We shall then be much more comfortable, for though in England this would be considered a homely residence, here it is thought a very good one.

We are allowed certain rations for six months, of meat, wheat, tea and sugar, sufficient for our family and servants. In respect of the situation, the nominal value of it is but five shillings a day, with rations for Hawkins and servant, but there are many advantages attached to it sufficient to supply the wants of our family and prevent our wanting any ready money for housekeeping. We live very well, get excellent fish, and the wild ducks are delicious. We are supplied with vegetables from the Government garden, and we are allowed the use of two cows, which, with two we have of our own, give us butter and milk. You must not judge of the produce of four cows here by what they give in England, for, being naturally wild, and the calves never weaned from them for fear they should not thrive so well, they can only be milked once a day. I am desired by Eliza and Mary to tell their cousin Ann they churned the first butter. The Government carts bring us a good supply of firewood, so that, altogether, my dear Ann, we have no reason to complain of our present situation, if retirement and seclusion from the world is not considered a trouble, which I am happy to say it is not. I often wish we could have beer and yeast to make bread, for not having the means of properly dressing our wheat, our bread is not English bread. Our candles we make ourselves.

Before I entirely take leave of the mountains I must tell you that the tree which we chained at the back of the last dray when descending the big hill was forty-eight feet long, and at the extremity, on the boughs, were seated three men. By this necessary precaution you will be enabled to judge better than I have described it to you the steepness and hazard for luggage to descend. Till bridges are thrown over the river, and the road much improved there can be little communication with this country, but that is to be done after [the governor] has crossed the mountains. The land on this side is so good for rearing cattle that nearly the whole consumption of the colony depends upon it, and many who cannot obtain land here are glad to send their cattle. In addition to our cavalcade, we had thirty-four head, which belonged to our landlord, on the following terms: One third of the produce to be ours, to be divided at the end of seven years. We have an increase of one calf since we have been here. Although we have not got our own land marked out for us yet, Hawkins has selected his spot, and applied for it, still until then we can

Mount Hay, Grose Valley

Mist in Grose Valley

Wet heathland near Blackheath

Cliffs of King's Tableland

have the use of as much as we want for any cattle we may possess.

I think there can be no doubt but we shall do well, and in a few years prosper; but I would never persuade any-one with a large family as mine, and slender means as we possessed, to leave England, for not one in a thousand could expect to be as fortunate as we have been, for without the appointment we have, and the assistance of the Government to bring us here, we never could have come, or without it we must have been subject to many hardships and privations that we have never felt. But I do wish that a few respectable fami-lies, who on their arrival here would be in possession of a few hundred or one thousand pounds, would come, for with such means they must do well—there can be nothing to pre-vent it.

The Commandant's eldest son took Tom last week to visit their men and cattle. They returned with a bullock to kill and put in store. Yesterday they again left us to be absent a week. He has huts on different parts of their land where their men reside who take care of their stock; at these huts they will rest at night, and he desired me to give his love to his cousin Tom, and to ask him how he would like to sleep before a large fire on a sheep-skin laid on bark, and in the day to go into the woods and hunt the kangaroos. He has gone away very happy, mounted on a large horse, accompanied by young Lawson and a man with seven or eight dogs, and he promised to bring home a kangaroo, an emu and a wild tur-key. We must encourage him in this kind of life, for in a few years I hope he will be of great service to us.

The greatest drawback in this country are the snakes, which are so extremely venomous that no person who has been bitten has been known to live many moments. They will not attack you unless molested. The only one I have seen was brought home by Tom the other day. It rose to bite the dog that barked at it, and the man killed it.

Tom and the children are all well; George is the most delicate; little Edward, the plaything of our leisure moments, and the darling of all. He has ever been a treasured babe from an idea that he was deprived of those little comforts attached to infants; he is a most healthy and lovely child, and it will be worthy of remark that, born in England, his first birthday was spent at Bathurst, the day on which his father took on himself the duties of commissariat. No child so young, I should think, ever travelled so far.

I hope, my dear friend, I have not wearied you in the perusal of this long letter, which has not been written without many interruptions, but I cannot undertake to correct its errors. And now, and for ever, may God bless you all.

Bathurst is 137 miles from Sydney, we were eighteen days on the road.

E. HAWKINS.

V

Barron Field

The eternal eucalyptus

Before coming to Australia the lawyer Barron Field was a contributor to the *Times* and the *Quarterly Review*. He was Judge of the Supreme Court of New South Wales from 1817 to 1824. This account of crossing the mountains in 1822 is taken from his *Geographical Memoirs on New South Wales*. Governor Macquarie liked Field, but British novelist and prime minister Benjamin Disraeli described him as 'noisy, obtrusive, jargonistic' and another observer called him a 'weak, silly man who fancied himself a poet born'.

Field's account is one of the finest examples of European snob writing about the Australian landscape to appear before D.H. Lawrence's justly more famous efforts, in his novel *Kangaroo*. As a general rule, the more educated and refined the sensibility of European observers, the more dimly have they been able to see while in Australia.

***

Monday, 7th October, 1822.
This spring month is the fittest to make this excursion in. The winter nights are too cold, and the summer days too

hot. In the autumn the flowers are not in bloom.

The difficulties of the travel commence at Emu Ford over the river Nepean, a branch of the Hawkesbury. Crossing this stream is always a work of such time and trouble, and sometimes of such difficulty and danger, that the traveller should send forward his cart or baggage-horses, to overcome it, half a day before he rides or rows through it himself. The ferry is the property of government, who have hitherto delayed either to provide a punt themselves or to suffer the stock-holders of the colony to build one by subscription. The consequences are frequent losses of cattle in swimming, and injury of sheep in boating, over. Although the river was not unusually high, we were obliged to unload our cart before it could be drawn through the ford, and thus lost several hours in transporting the baggage by one small boat, and in reloading the cart.

On the banks of the Nepean, I saw almost the only deciduous native tree in the territory, namely, the white cedar ... All the other indigenous trees and shrubs that I have seen are evergreens: the eternal eucalyptus, with its white bark and its scanty tin-like foliage, or the dark casuarina tall, and exocarpus funeral; all as unpicturesque as the shrubs and flowers are beautiful ... New South Wales is a perpetual flower garden, but there is not a single scene in it of which a painter could make a landscape, without greatly disguising the true character of the trees. They have no lateral boughs, and cast no masses of shade; but in return, it is to this circumstance, which causes so little vegetable putrefaction, that the healthiness of the climate is mainly to be attributed. 'A part of the economy' (says Mr. Brown the botanist) 'which contributes somewhat to the peculiar character of the Australian forests, is, that the leaves both of the eucalyptus and acacia, by far the most common genera in Terra Australis, and, if taken together, and considered with respect to the mass of vegetable matter they contain (calculated from the size, as well as the number of individuals) nearly equal to all the other plants of that country, are vertical, or present their margin and not either surface towards the stem, both surfaces having consequently the same relation to light.' Can this circumstance be partly the cause of their unpicturesqueness—of the monotony of their leaf? Or is it merely their evergreenness? 'In the Indies' (says Linnaeus) 'almost all the trees are evergreen, and have broad leaves; but in our cold regions, most trees cast their foliage every year, and such as do not, bear acerose, that is, narrow and acute, leaves. If they were broader, the snow which falls during the winter would collect among them, and break the branches by its weight. Their great slenderness prevents any such effect, and allows the snow to pass between them.' But snow is not unknown to the eucalypti and acaciae of New Holland; and may not the verticalness of the broad leaves of some of them answer the same snow-diverting purpose as the acerose-leavedness of European evergreens? ...

Be this as it may, no tree, to my taste, can be beautiful that is not deciduous. What can a painter do with one cold olive-green? There is a dry harshness about the perennial leaf, that does not savour of humanity in my eyes. There is no flesh and blood in it; it is not of us, and is nothing to us. Dryden says of the laurel:

> *From winter winds it suffers no decay;*
> *For ever fresh and fair, and every month is May.*

Now it may be the fault of the cold climate in which I was bred, but this is just what I complain of in an evergreen. 'For ever fresh,' is a contradiction in terms; what is 'for ever fair' is never fair; and without January, in my mind, there can be no May. All the dearest allegories of human life are bound up in the infant and slender green of spring, the dark redundance of summer, and the sere and yellow leaf of autumn. These are as essential to the poet as emblems, as they are to the painter as picturesque objects; and the common consent and immemorial custom of European poetry have made the change of seasons, and its effect upon vegetation, a part, as it were, of our very nature. I can therefore hold no fellowship with Australian foliage, but will cleave to the British oak through all the bareness of winter ... 'New Holland' (says Sir James Smith) 'seems no very beautiful or picturesque country, such as is likely to form, or to inspire, a poet. Indeed the dregs of the community, which we have poured upon its shores, must probably subside and purge themselves, before anything like a poet, or a disinterested lover of nature, can arise from so foul a source. There seems, however, to be no transition of seasons in the climate itself, to excite hope, or to expand the heart and fancy.'

Yet let me do justice to the evergreens of New Holland. It is to the scantiness of their foliage that the grazier owes the dry wholesomeness of the native grasses, however thin; and it is to the undecaying and aromatic, myrtaceous, perennial leaf that the colonists attribute the healthiness of their climate. No miasmata come from the marshes or fallen leaves of Australian forests. Intermittent fevers are unknown here … The climate of New South Wales is becoming generally cooler, as the colony gets cleared of timber … it is important to agriculture that I should mention that the stumps of the eucalypti, from the quantity of gum they contain, do not rot in the ground soon after the trees have been cut down, as those of the American and Norfolk Island timbers do. They must be grubbed up, or burnt out by piling the surrounding sods over them, like a kiln.

At Emu Plains or Island (for it is sometimes insulated by the washings of the mountains, when the Nepean is flooded) there is a government agricultural establishment of 350 men and a few women, with a good brick house for the superintendent, and wooden huts for the convict labourers. Here are grown for the benefit of the crown, wheat, maize and tobacco; but experience everywhere proves the loss at which government raises its own supplies. These plains are not naturally cleared; but they will soon be free from stumps by the labour of these convicts, and will then leave a rich tract of arable land for favoured grantees.

It is this river, whether we call it Hawkesbury or Nepean, that is the Nile of Botany Bay; for the land on its banks owes its fertility to the floods which come down from the Blue Mountains, and which have been known to swell the waters nearly a hundred feet above their usual level; and as these floods are uncertain and often destructive of the growing crops, I once thought that government (if it is to farm at all) had better have kept the whole of this precarious garden in its own hands; since it is only public foresight that would provide against the loss of a harvest, and only public wealth that could support it. After the flood of 1817, the government ration was reduced from eleven to three pounds of wheat per week; but since that period so much wheat has been grown in the fine districts of Appin and Airds, and in the island of Van Diemen's Land, that the colony is now almost independent of these flood-farmers; and they are yearly going out of fashion, for the benefit of the state.

Nothing can be more uncertain than the heavy rains of the climate. Sometimes (but not of late years) the country is worse afflicted with long droughts, in which the woods take fire and consume the grass, and the cattle have perished for want of water. Often do the rains descend, and the floods come, when the Hawkesbury corn is in the ground, and the colony has suffered from the improvidence of these farmers, in not building their wheat stacks out of the reach of the devouring waters. The extraordinary fertility of these flooded lands, which have borne a crop of wheat and a crop of maize in each year for the last five-and-twenty years, has naturally induced their tenants to rely too much upon this lubberland sort of farming ... Another good reason against granting away this land, and suffering it to be cleared, is, that the floods wash the fallen timber into the channel of the river, and obstruct the navigation. The removal of the trees from its banks has not only contributed to choke the river by their falling in, but has occasioned derelictions on one side and alluvions on the other.

But we shall never get our cart up Lapstone Hill at this rate; and it is so steep and long, that we were obliged to shift our baggage twice in ascending it, notwithstanding Governor Macquarie's Government and General Order of the 10th June, 1815, says, that 'the facility of the ascent to Spring Wood excited surprise, and is certainly not well calculated to give the traveller a just idea of the difficulties he has afterwards to encounter.' I found Lapstone Hill as difficult as any in the journey, except Mount York; and we did not reach Spring Wood (twelve miles and a half from the river), where alone there is a space enough in the forest to encamp upon, till after nine o'clock at night. There is little or no grass here, and the timber consists principally of those species of eucalyptus called by the colonists stringy and iron-bark. Here is stationed an acting corporal's party of the 48th regiment, in a small barrack.

Tuesday, 8th October.
Set forward at half an hour after nine o'clock, am, and halted on a mossy sand-hill above Jamison Valley, two miles beyond King's Tableland, at five o'clock pm, having travelled sixteen miles this day. This station is now called The Burnt Weatherboard Hut [just beyond Katoomba] and was Governor Macquarie's second depot for making the road. The timber now became more dwarf, and we were actually crossing the Blue Mountains. We found the pass very alpine and difficult, rocky, sandy, stony, flowery. The views were very grand. The night was stormy, but little rainy—all in the sublime. 'The power of hills was on me,' as Wordsworth says. I could not sleep for thinking of our situation, and walked forth from my tent. The air was refreshing. All were asleep from fatigue, with large fires of piled wood at their feet, the gleams of which (for they had been suffered to go down) gave a picturesque effect to the tent and cart, and to the tethered horses, which were patiently standing on the bleak and bare hill. A little more than thirty years ago, this land was inhabited by savages only, and these hills had, from the beginning of time, formed an impassable barrier between their tribes. The spirit of British government had now come from the antipodes, and, with nothing but a colony of convicts, had, in that short time, penetrated upwards of a hundred miles into the interior of the country, and established a township there, to which the unarmed might travel as safely as from London to Bristol.

The very sleeping grooms beneath me had been thieves and robbers, and the blasted heath looked like New Hounslow; but our persons and property were inviolate.

Wednesday, 9th October.
Moved at 8.30 am, and arrived at the bottom of Cox's Pass down Mount York at 5.30 pm, (twenty-one miles and a half). The ridge of mountains (or rather rocks), along which this passage could alone be effected, is very difficult and desolate. The trees (still eucalyptus) are stunted and burnt, with the exception of one light species called the ash, of which good white-coopers' work might be made, and perhaps ships' smaller spars. The King's Tableland is as anarchial and untabular as any His Majesty possesses. The Prince Regent's Glen below it (if it be the glen that I saw) is not very romantic. Jamison Valley we found by no means a happy one. Blackheath is a wretched misnomer. Not to mention its awful contrast to that beautiful place of that name in England, heath it is none. Black it may be when the shrubs are burnt, as they often are. Pitt's Amphitheatre disappointed me. The hills are thrown together in a monotonous manner, and their clothing is very unpicturesque—a mere sea of harsh trees; but Mr. Pitt was no particular connoisseur either in mountain scenery or in amphitheatres. Mount York (as Governor Macquarie named it) redeems the journey across the Blue Mountains, for it leads you to the first green valley. The earliest burst of Christian transalpine country, as seen from the beginning of this mountain, is very beautiful. The sight of grass again is lovely. The view from the commencement of Cox's Pass down to it, is finer still. This Big Hill, as it is alone called, should have been named Mount Pisgah, for it affords the first view of the promised land of Australia, after the wilderness of the Blue Mountains ...

Thursday, 10th October.
Did not proceed until half past 9 am, but performed twenty-one miles this day, and encamped on the banks of the Fish River at 7 pm. This is the first stream that flows westerly,

Cox's River falling into the Nepean. The journey today was all beautiful. Cox's River (five miles from his pass down Mount York, which might be avoided by an easier and shorter road to the north of it) is worth going to spend a few days at, of itself. It is a pretty stream, and rich in the botanical and picturesque. Here the first granite is seen ...

Here we met a few Indian natives of Bathurst. They resembled the natives of the coast in appearance, but did not speak the same language. They seem, however, to have advanced towards civilization one degree further than the poor forked animals of the warmer climate, inasmuch as they possess the art of very neatly sewing together, with the sinews of the kangaroo and emu, cloaks of skins, the hide of which they also carve in the inside with a world of figures. They use these cloaks for the sole purpose of keeping themselves warm, and have as little sense of decency as the natives around Sydney; for in the middle of the day, when the weather is warm, they throw back their cloaks across their shoulders. They appear to be a harmless race with nothing ferocious in their manners or countenance. They are perfectly cheerful, laughing at every thing they see, and repeating every thing they hear. For the rest, little can be added to Captain Tench's and Colonel Collins' accounts of the natives of New South Wales. Their numbers are diminishing. Not that they retreat before the settlements of Europeans; this they cannot do; the different tribes (few as their numbers are) would resist the invasion of each other's territory. Thirty or forty miles will reach the circumference of each family's peregrinations. The tribes about our first settlements are as ignorant of the country beyond the mountains as the colonists were; and such is the sterility of the greater part of Mr. Oxley's first interior route, that he met with only twenty-two Indians in a journey of five months.

Of the persons of the natives of New South Wales, I think Colonel Collins has given too unfavourable a picture. Their faces have generally (in my opinion) too much goodnature to be absolutely hideous, and (to my taste) they do not imitate humanity so abominably as the African negroes. Their hair is not woolly; their heads are not dog-like; nor are their legs baboonish. The figure of many of them is very good; and, as for their leanness, how can they wax fat in so poor a country? From the neighbourhood of our settlement we have scared the kangaroo and the emu, and left these poor lords of the creation no created food but a few opossums, and a tenancy in common with us of fish. Together with their numbers, their customs and manners are in a state of decay. The ceremony of extracting one of the right upper front teeth from the jaw of adults (so fully described by Colonel Collins) is nearly obsolete in the neighbourhood of our settlements, and the custom is by no means universal in the island. But the *corrobory*, or night-dance, still obtains. This festivity is performed in very good time, and not unpleasing tune. The song is sung by a few males and females who take part in the dance. One of the band beats time by knocking one stick against another. The music begins with a high note, and gradually sinks to the octave, whence it rises again immediately to the top ... The dancers breathe in chorus like paviours, and the general step consists in opening the knees with a convulsive shake to the music; but occasionally they thread the mazes of each other, without any confusion. They stripe themselves down the waist, and paint their faces with white clay and red ochre, and in compliment to European delicacy, wear boughs round their loins. The glare of the large fires gives a picturesque effect to the savage scene, and the dance works up the performers to a sublime enthusiasm.

I have been thus minute, because in a few years, perhaps, even the corrobory will be no more, so sophisticated do the Indians become from their pernicious association with the convicts, who sow seeds of drunkenness in the prolific soil of savage indolence. A rum, or even sugar-cask, filled with water, furnishes these poor creatures with an intoxicating liquor; and the invasions of civilization are reproached with the introduction of a new vice, which operates as an inflamer of all their old ones. It is a melancholy sight to witness the drunken quarrels and fightings of the simple natives of Australia, in the streets of Sydney—a people to whom civilization can never bring the comforts of food, raiment and shelter, and the blessings of religion, as an atonement for the vice and disease which it necessarily carries along with it. That these unfortunate beings were comparatively ignorant of the crime of evil-speaking before we came among them, is proved by the broken English words of scurrility and execration with which they pollute their native tongue. The effect of this would be ludicrous, were not the cause pitiable. Truly Botany Bay is a bad school for them; but they have not learnt of the convicts to lie or to steal. Perhaps it is better that their name should pass away from the earth. They will not serve, and they are too indolent and poor in spirit to become masters. They would always be drones in the hive of an industrious colony. Nevertheless they are not without the stamp of their Maker's image, cut in ebony (as old Fuller says) instead of ivory. They bear themselves erect, and address you with confidence, always with good-humour, and often with grace. They are not common beggars, although they accept of our carnal things in return for the fish and oysters, which are almost all we have left them for their support. They are the Will Wimbles of the colony; the carriers of news and fish; the gossips of the town; the loungers on the quay. They know of everybody's business, although they have none of their own—but this. They give a locality to the land, and their honest naked simplicity affords relief to the eye from the hypocritical lour [sullen look] of the yellow-clad convict.

The warlike features of the tribes which surround our settlements are now quite effaced. The savages are forbidden to enter the towns with their spears, and they cheerfully comply with this requisition. They have a bowing acquaintance with everybody, and scatter their *How-d'ye-do's* with an air of friendliness and equality, and with a perfect English accent, undebased by the *Massa's* and *Missies,* and *me'no's* of West Indian slavery. They have been tried to be brought up from infancy as servants, but they have always run away to the woods. Our government has also instituted a small school for the education of native black children. Some of their parents (particularly of half-castes) have no objection to their being clothed, and fed, and taught; but they cannot endure the thoughts of their being made servants. The children learn almost readily as Europeans; but their parents will steal them away when they grow up, and they will not willingly return among us. A few pairs have been married and housed out of the school, but they will not settle.

The *Sydney Gazette* used to make a great puffing about Governor Macquarie's Native Institution. Since his departure the school has been very properly removed from the town of Parramatta, to a remoter situation in the interior, on the Richmond Road; but when I visited it in 1823 there were but four children in the school of the whole Indian blood, and four tenants of the settling-huts erected for them by the government; and of these last (although it was the day of the committee's quarterly meeting) only one was at home; but I was told they attended more numerously once a fortnight to receive their ration from the government store. The few children of the half-blood are the results of 'casual fruition'. Great as is the disproportion of white women to men, there is no instance of even a convict permanently living with a black woman; so that there will be no class of creoles in Australia.

Their instinctive relish for the vermin and range of the woods cannot be eradicated. 'Sir' (said Dr. Johnson, holding up a slice from a quartern loaf) 'this is better than the bread-fruit', but the savages of Australia, although extremely fond of bread, will never lose their more exquisite relish for a fine fat grub. 'Poor Tom! that eats the swimming frog, the toad, the tadpole, the wall-newt and the water; swallows the old rat, and the ditch-dog; drinks the green mantle of the standing pool. But let us talk with this philosopher.' If he is the most independent who has the fewest wants, the houseless Australian is certainly our superior: 'He owes the worm no silk, the beast no hide, the sheep no wool, the cat no perfume'; he looks upon us as 'sophisticated' but he always treats our persons with respect, although he holds our servants very cheap, and looks down with a kind of stoical pity upon the various articles of comfort to which we have made ourselves slaves. He has no notion of that inferiority to us, the oppression of which feeling reduces the New Zealanders and South Sea Islanders almost to despair; and he despises the comforts of civilization, although he has nothing of his own but his hollow tree and liberty, without even the 'crust of bread'. What then must be his opinion of our servants?—men and women, who sacrifice their liberty and independence for the second-rate comforts of civilization, which they earn by submitting to perform menial offices for those who enjoy first-rate, and by ministering to their artificial wants; for even which first-rate comforts the naked native has a contempt. With us masters, all he contends for nevertheless is equality. He acknowledges the British government, and even accepts from the governor grants of his own patrimonial land.

Some of the Indians have also seriously applied to be allowed convict-labourers, as the settlers are, although they have no patience to remain in the huts which our government has built for them, till the maize and cabbages that have been planted to their hands are fit to gather. So the Spaniards succeeded at length in domesticating many of the negroes of the Philippine Islands, and converting them to Christianity, to which they made no objection so long as they received subsistence; but when they were obliged to labour for the maintenance of their family, they returned to the mountains. We have now lived among the Australians more than thirty years; and yet, like the North American Indians, or the negroes of the Philippine Islands, they have adopted none of our arts of life, with the exception of exchanging their stone hatchets and shell fish-hooks for our iron ones. They will never become builders, or cultivators, or mechanics, or mariners, like the New Zealanders or the South Sea Islanders, nor indeed till they cease to be at all, will they ever be other than they are.

When all thy simple race is extinct, thy name, gentle and well-bred Harry! shall be recorded, at least, in the pages of this journal.

Our courtiers say all's savage but at court.

But of this, at least, I am sure, that thou wert the most cour-
teous savage that ever bade good-morrow. Compliments are
difficult things to an unpractised tongue, but thou wert naturally polite; and I owe thee at least this poor return for the
grace and dignity of thy compliments. And thou too, Cogy!
never shall I forget thy intoxicating laugh; and the recollec-
tion of thy good-humoured face will come across me in other
climes and at distant days, like a picture that will never lose its
interest. Very pleasant wert thou to me, Cogy, when pleas-
ures with me were very rare.

After leaving Cox's River, we ascended a very steep hill called
Mount Blaxland, and saw Wentworth's and Lawson's Sugar-
loaves, as Governor Macquarie called them. They are mere
hummocks—lumps of sugar. These three gentlemen, namely,
Messrs. Gregory Blaxland, William Wentworth, and Lieutenant Lawson, of the Royal Veteran Company, are exclu-
sively entitled to the merit of exploring this pass over the
barrier mountains of the colony, and therefore ought to have
been more substantially rewarded, than by a mere grant of
one thousand acres each of the country they discovered, and
the sugar-plum of a name. In this attempt Lieutenant Dawes,
Captain Tench, Hacking, Ensign Barrallier of the 102nd regiment, the enterprising Mr. Bass, and Mr. Caley the botanist,
had successively failed. When Messrs. Blaxland, Wentworth
and Lawson returned home only for want of provisions, then
Governor Macquarie sends forth Mr. Deputy Surveyor Evans,
who very naturally sees the next high hill and calls it Evans'
Peak, or Crown, and pushes on to Bathurst Plains; and the
journals and geographies talk of the discoveries of Mr. Evans
and Governor Macquarie ...

    The quiet of a beautiful night on the banks of the
Fish River led me to remark on 'rural sounds'. The notes of
the birds of New Holland are rather cries than songs, but
many of them are pleasing and plaintive. Some are harsh and
vulgar, like those of the parrot-kind, the cockatoo, and coachman's whip-bird, the bell-bird (which I call the creaking-
wheel-bird), the razor grinder, and the laughing jackass (a

series [species] of kingfisher); but a sort of cuckoo-noted bird
sings at night, something between the voice of the English
cuckoo and the bark of a watch-dog. The river treated us
with a frog-concert all night—a constant common croaking,
timed by bass-notes, like a deep sheep-bell, or the human
voice. The Fish River is not so picturesque as Cox's; but it is
a full and rapid stream, with rippling falls, and equally rich in
flowers. The fish would not bite, but we shot a wood-duck
for breakfast. Here we killed a brown snake, about six feet
long …

Saturday, 12th October.
Rain, which came on last evening, set in to-day, and detained us at this farm till noon, when the weather cleared up,
and the evening proved beautiful. Our road now lay over a
succession of plains, still more clear and fine than O'Connell
Plains. These are called Macquarie Plains and Bathurst Plains.
In the former, the Fish River joins the Macquarie. Arrived
in good time at the town of Bathurst. Here we set up our
rest, and pitched our tent for the Sabbath, on the naturally
cleared land of the winding banks of the Macquarie, which
are here and there edged with a few swamp oaks (*Casuarina
paludosa*). I could hardly believe I was travelling in New Holland this day; so differently—so English—is the character of
the scenery—downs, meadows and streams in the flat—no
side-scenes of eucalyptus …

The scarcity of wood now takes away the American
log-appearance of the cottages; they build of turf here, and
roof with straw or reeds, instead of wooden shingles. You
may see as far as the eye can reach. Stockmen, cattle and
sheep occasionally form your horizon, as in Old Holland—a
Paul Potter or Cuyp effect rare in New Holland. At sunset
we saw wooded hills, distant enough to display that golden
blue or purple which landscape-painters love. The smoke of
the little village of Bathurst is seen for miles off, which that
of no other town in Australia is. These things may seem trifling to an English reader; but by an American or Australian,
accustomed to travel through the eternal valley of the shadow

of monotonous woods, the charm of emerging into anything like European scenery will be duly appreciated ...

Sunday, 13th October.
An English Sabbath-morning—heavy mist slowly rolling away, lingering with a light cloud across the tops of the hills. The principal chaplain of the colony (the Rev. Samuel Marsden) who happened to be here on a visit, performed divine service in the government granary (a large brick building) to about sixty people, including soldiers and convicts. After service, I visited a few of the small settlers' huts, and found the parents cleanly, and the children even more expensively drest. Rum, the bane of colonies, has scarcely yet found its way over the mountains, and happily the town of Bathurst is not yet large enough to support a public-house. The afternoon proved stormy, and the night rainy ...

Friday, 18th October.
Cloudy and windy morning, but the rain kept off for the day. Returned to Bathurst, by a shorter route, through another of Evans's Plains, to the westward of Queen Charlotte's Valley. The first half of this division was highly romantic, the creek winding at the base of hills through large, scattered and piled masses of rock, forming little falls and strong ripples. The second half lay over Evans's clear plain—a fine country, but not so well watered or so beautiful as Queen Charlotte's Valley. Dined at a large settler's farm, on the other side of the Macquarie River, near Bathurst. There was an English air of neatness about the homesteads and paddocks. Some of these were matted with English grasses, and stocked with fine-woolled sheep, and lambs as big as sheep ...

Friday, 25th October.
The rain came in the night with wind. Took my final departure this morning, and reached home soon after noon, having travelled three hundred miles in less than three weeks. It now only remains for me to express my thorough satisfaction, that this fine transalpine country will be the making of

the colony of New South Wales, and will give it a decided superiority over that of Van Diemen's Land. 'The general description of these heretofore unexplored regions' (says Governor Macquarie) 'given by Mr. Evans (himself the deputy surveyor of Van Diemen's Land), is, that they very far surpass in beauty and fertility of soil any that he has seen in New South Wales or Van Diemen's Land.' If they had not been discovered, grazing, from which alone the state can derive an export, must have come to a stop. Here is an opening for English migrants for centuries; and I have not a doubt that, in spite of the want of navigable rivers, New Holland will be a second America.

VI

X.Y.Z.

The western road is the romantic road

The lively letters from which the following extracts are taken appeared in the *Australian* newspaper in 1827, signed 'X.Y.Z.'. (The *Australian* newspaper of that time is not related to the one we have today.) Historian Malcolm Ellis has suggested they were written by Captain William Dumaresque, brother-in-law of Governor Ralph Darling and the colony's inspector of roads and bridges. As can be seen from his comments on government farms, the author, whoever he was, was an early advocate of privatization. Some of his comments on nature, such as his guess that a particular waterfall was two thousand feet high, were fanciful.

The final extract is notable for the writer's conviction that Aborigines had just told Europeans around Bathurst of the existence of an inland sea. Presumably these accounts of the ocean originated with Aborigines living on the Indian Ocean or elsewhere on the coast, and were passed from tribe to tribe until they reached the people of central New South Wales.

The western road is the romantic road, because it leads direct to the Blue Mountains, to Bathurst, and thence the Lord knows where. We all know it begins in George Street, but who shall determine where it stops? ...

The Sydney toll-gate is in point of convenience and architectural embellishment quite unique, but being in the Gothic style is perhaps rather too light for the rough purposes of a public turnpike, although it would look admirably as the entrance lodge to some of the colonial parks of our richest settlers. It is decidedly the Hyde Park Corner of our western road, and with the addition of some well arranged lamps might safely bear a comparison with that celebrated, gay and bustling entrance into London. [The toll gate was in what is now Railway Square.] The ill-natured remarks that were once made about this pretty trifle of Governor Macquarie's appear now perfectly contemptible. He looked to the gradual advancement of the colony and built accordingly. Though the old gentleman was charged with wasting the public money in a lavish taste for useless buildings of mere ornament, it is due to his memory to say that every structure in or near Sydney, affording to the eye of taste the least pleasure or satisfaction, are all Macquarie's. The public buildings around this toll-gate are the Benevolent Asylum, a large spacious and handsome building for the reception of the old and infirm poor, supported by voluntary contributions, standing in a fine healthy situation, and productive by its good management of the greatest good to Sydney, where such a thing as a beggar is never seen; the other is called the Carters' Barracks, an extensive government establishment, containing a large tread-mill, for the punishment of refractory prisoners, while the principal part of the building is devoted to the reformation of the juvenile offenders transported from England and Ireland. These young delinquents appear to be treated in the most affectionate and tender manner; their health and morals are not only the most carefully attended to, but they have all the advantages of good teachers in their school, which lasts six hours a day. No school in England can boast of such an ample playground as these young rogues enjoy after their roast beef and New Testament is over; and when one rides past, and sees them in all the hilarity of youthful mirth, enjoying the government swings and playing at cricket, bat and ball, leap-frog and prisoners' base, it never occurs to the spectator that these can possibly be the identical urchins who have so much infested the London streets of late years, and given the Recorder of London such trouble when they have been arraigned before him at the Old Bailey. Now they are in a fair way of beginning the world *de novo* and are likely to turn out honest men.

On the right is the elegant and hospitable mansion called Ultimo House, which will not only be remembered by hundreds in the colony, but by many officers of rank in England and India, who have formerly partaken of its crowded entertainments. On the opposite side of the road about half a mile off stands one of the best built houses of the colony, called Cleveland House, and farther on, at the bottom of the hill, are the extensive flour mills, granaries and distillery of one of the most industrious men in New South Wales; £20,000 is said to have been already expended on these works, which are on a scale of magnitude that would do credit to London itself. We now get completely out of town, and the pretty little white circular building at intervals along the road, with a board hanging outside stating 'A constable here' explain what they are intended for, and give the passenger assurances of safe travelling. Here is a picturesque English-looking farm belonging to the King, called Grose Farm [now the grounds of Sydney University]. His Majesty's father of sacred memory, King George the third, was a great farmer, and took much pleasure in affecting the life of a gentleman farmer at his retreat at Kew; but his son, his present gracious Majesty, King George the fourth, far excels him in his love of farming, as would appear by the excessive number of fine farms he keeps in cultivation in New South Wales. This Grose Farm is the first of them, but I never understood that it pays its expenses. At the four mile stone is our Ascot heath, where at the autumn and October meetings may be seen assembled four or five thousand of the Sydney folk to witness the races. With the exception of the celebrated course just mentioned, Epsom, Doncaster, York, and a few others, such as Chester, Newcastle, and Preston, Sydney race course presents as good a turn out as any in England. Five or six coaches and four, one or two tandems, half a dozen curricles, besides gigs, and riding horses, almost innumerable, convince you that you are in anything but a poor country. Adjoining is the pretty estate of Annandale, belonging to the family of the late Colonel Johnstone. The orange and lemon groves of this estate are equal to those of the Queen's garden in Lisbon.

At the five mile stone, the road turns off to the left, to Liverpool, the Cow Pastures, and the rich County of Argyle. After passing several well enclosed and partially improved properties belonging to gentlemen engaged in business all the day in Sydney, we arrive at a pretty farm called Long-bottom, but find, upon enquiry, it is the king's. The establishment appears small, but for what purpose of public utility it is maintained, small as it is, nobody could inform me. The road continues good all the way, and enables the stage coaches going to and from Sydney to make up, by a gallop, the usual time lost when changing horses. Passing Homebush and Newington, two extensive and valuable estates belonging to bank directors in Sydney, we leave the pretty town of Parramatta on the right hand, and proceed due west for the Blue Mountains. The Government Domain and Toongabbie extend four or five miles along the road, till one comes to Prospect Hill, where a rich black vegetable mould is seen to the top of the hill, which has been cropped, with good profit, over the very summit, these twenty years, without a single load of manure. Such a fact would appear incredible in England. This estate comprises an extent of three thousand acres, entirely fenced in with a five rail fence, and it does one good to see its style of old English hospitality kept up within the house. One hundred bales of fine wool were ready for shipment, being this year's shearing from ten thousand sheep belonging to the worthy proprietor. On the opposite side of the road at Prospect is the estate of Flushcombe, the owner of which is said to have made one thousand pounds by the first year's services of his fine English horse, Camerton ... Passing the *gentle master Slender's* one comes to Rooty Hill, another enormous farm, belonging to His Majesty, of three thousand acres. The establishment here is on a considerable scale; and the labourers, like the numerous horses kept to breed by the government, seem to have nothing to do but to eat, drink and enjoy themselves.

On the high part of the road here we first got a peep at the Blue Mountains, and we trotted on in order to reach our resting place at Springwood before dark ... Beyond Minchinbury and Mount Druitt, two well cultivated and eligible farms, there is a considerable descent in the road to the south creek, over which there is a low bridge, frequently flooded in the rainy season ... The south creek can boast of a number of rich and substantial settlers, who, making their farms home *stations,* have their large flocks and herds depasturing over the mountains—some in Argyle, and some at Hunter's River. The immense and certain profits of breeding stock in those fine countries have raised to wealth and independence many in this neighbourhood, who, but for their sheep and cattle, must have remained in their original obscurity. Now their houses are furnished with all good things in abundance, at whatever price, and two or three hundred pounds is not considered an object for the advantages of sending a son a voyage to England, for the benefit of a good education. At Penrith, on the banks of the Nepean River, we refreshed ourselves and horses at the hospitable quarters of a friend, in the commission of France, who can show some of the most substantial farm buildings to the colony.

We were now thirty-five miles from Sydney, a long ride in the heat of the day, and having ten or twelve miles further, we hurried away, and, for a shilling a piece, the punt carried us all across the river to Emu Plains, one of the most fertile and beautiful tracts of country in the colony. Here is about four thousand acres of rich alluvial flat, but it is in the hands of His Majesty, who is a prodigious grower of wheat and cobs of corn on these plains. This is a very large establishment, and used to be a sort of minor penal settlement, but I believe it is now nothing but an agricultural farm, for the raising of wheat. For what purpose it is impossible to say. It was light enough to count twenty-three stacks of last year's crop, not yet threshed out, still standing in the field, besides a much larger number of stacks, which I could not count, of new wheat. What it is all for, I cannot imagine. While the market price of wheat continues at 3s. 6d. to 5s. per bushel, the loss at such establishments must be enormous. It needs no ghost to come from the grave to tell us the disadvantages which large government establishments labour under, in such a country as New South Wales, compared with the hard working settler, who can hardly get a living, although working with his own hands, unless he has sheep or cattle in addition to his land in tillage. By a very moderate calculation, I consider the loss of this government farm at Emu a dead loss to the public of three thousand five hundred a year, and the more they grow, the greater the loss. One man's loss is often another's gain, but here it is quite the reverse, for the more the government loses in this unworthy competition with the poor devil of a settler, in the raising of wheat and maize, the sooner is the settler ruined by the market being shut against him.

I think I see you walking your horse between His Majesty's superb Lodge, and the margin of Virginia Water, certainly one of the sweetest spots in all England, and illustrative of the excellent good taste so conspicuous in the King. Now let us suppose an impossibility: that a thousand acres of land were ordered to be ploughed up there, and cultivated with wheat, by 250 men, from the hulks at Woolwich, for the use of the army and navy of Great Britain. What would the jolly farmers say the next market day at Staines? And what would Mr. Hume and his tribe say in the House of Commons, of such a misuse of the public labour? And his Grace the Minister of the Ordnance would soon be about their ears, that his public works, roads, and wharfs, at Sheerness, should be interrupted, because the workmen had been drawn off to grow wheat at Virginia Water as if his Majesty could not buy it at one quarter the price he could possibly grow it. At a time when two thousand applications for crown servants remain unsatisfied for want of prisoners, and both plough and farming improvements are almost at a standstill for want of hands in many places in the colony of New South Wales it cannot but be lamented that so many of those assignable crown prisoners should be reserved in the hands of the superintendents of farming establishments at Emu and elsewhere. I saw four men wheeling an empty wheel-barrow, two before and two behind, at the rate of about one mile in two hours, and I could not help regretting they were not at Hunter's River, where men are so much wanted. But we must get up the hill—this sermonizing will never do ...

The first ascent of the Blue Mountains, by this new Lapstone Hill, is excellent. It would be perfectly practicable to take over, as I said before, a train of twenty-four pounders. Many generations however, must pass away before this will be seen in New South Wales; but it would, notwithstanding, be a fine sight to see fifty bullocks harnessed to a gun marching in array up the bristling hill. It took us nearly an hour to reach the top, and as the sun had just dipped behind the top of the range of mountains, we could only take a hasty glance at the magnificent view below us. Looking towards Sydney and the sea, the whole County of Cumberland lay extended at our feet. To the north were the hamlets of Castlereagh, Richmond and Wilberforce, and the town of Windsor, till the eye stretching over this fertile country, this Egypt of Australia, lost itself in the exhalations from the Hawkesbury, which as evening came on, were condensing over the whole line of its course. In front was the ferry which we had just crossed, and a thick, dark-looking forest, that soon terminated the view to the eastward, while immediately below was a fine bird's eye view of Emu Plains, without a tree—the neat cottage of the Superintendent, and the filthy bark huts or barracks of the men, together with those of fifteen thousand bushels of wheat grown by government contained in stacks almost too small for sight.

On the right hand, and on a fine foreground, stood the palace of Regentville, the noble seat of Sir John Jamison. This splendid building is beyond all comparisons, the finest thing of the kind in New South Wales; it stands on the top of a gentle hill, and presents a front to the long reach of the river and rich vale of Emu, of 180 feet; the centre building being eighty feet in length, and the two wings fifty each. In the wings are comprised the library, baths, billiard-rooms, &c., &c.; while the kitchens and servants offices are detached in the rear, out of sight. Regentville is built of a fine free stone, dug on the estate, in the chastest style of Grecian architecture, and is no less remarkable in the *interior* for the good taste and richness of its decorations, and the profuse and constant hospitality of the noble owner.

Opposite is the picturesque and romantic retreat of Edenglassie, while further to the south are the hills of the Cow Pastures and Argyle, which from their great elevation soon shut in the view. Emu Plains seems the very place for a town, and it is wonderful for what reason its eligibility should have been so long neglected. In a picturesque and fertile valley of eight or ten thousand acres, the succulency of whose soil would produce any thing and everything, with a noble river running through the midst, and at a convenient distance from Sydney and Parramatta—the town of Emu, with its church and spire, its court-house and its smithy, with a happy and ruddy peasantry for miles around, will soon, I hope succeed to these miserable stacks of wheat ...

We now rode on for Springwood, and had an unpleasant ride the last six or seven miles in the dark, the road not being here so good, many stumps being left standing in the middle, on which my tired horse made a frequent stumble. From Sydney to Springwood in one day is no joke, to one not accustomed to the saddle; and I thought this ten or twelve miles in the dark, longer than all the rest of the journey put together. Once or twice, from the blackness of the night, and the narrowness of the road, I got into the bush, till suddenly brought up by a thick scrub, which the horse could not penetrate, or receiving a knock on the head from an impending bough, I was obliged to exert my lungs and cooey out for my companion, who *cooeyed* in return, and by the sound of his voice I was enabled to find my way back to the road. I thought we should never get to Springwood, and from the horrid length of the miles, had I been asked at the moment how I liked the Blue Mountains, I must certainly have answered with Majochi, 'Piu no que si' ['More no than yes']. At last the yelping of some dozen angry curs, resounding through the silent forest, gave symptoms of the abode of man—it must be Springwood—but it was a miserable melancholy hole—not a glimmer of a light of any kind shone askaunt the lofty trees, and but for the noisy dogs we might have passed it in the dark. I got off my saddle with a slight groan, and was soon convinced by the dark dungeon appearance of the place we were not exactly on the Bath road. 'How many *quarts* of corn shall I give your horse?' said a private of the 57th regiment, one of the road party under charge of a corporal usually stationed at this first stage of the mountain road. I had previously heard that our horses would be very badly off going over the mountains, but I was not prepared to hear of corn being sold by the quart. I thought I could do no better than refer the good-natured soldier to the horse himself, and requested he might have for his supper as much as he could eat. When the baggage came up we got some slices of ham fried, and by the help of a bottle of port, some cigars, and brandy and water, from our own stock, we made a tolerable supper, and lay down in our clothes till daylight.

Some dirty pork fat or dripping, in a bit of broken plate, was our only lamp, and just before the last *flare*, which we had delayed by a great deal of coaxing of the cotton as long as possible, I discovered a large white tarantula, about the size of a dollar, just over my head, upon a piece of cotton that served as a curtain to the couch or bed, outside of which we lay. We had made up our minds to fleas and bugs in quantity, and were not disappointed, but had made no reckoning for any of the spider species; my companion therefore seized a fork to run this tarantula through, but though an excellent shot in general, missed his aim, and the tarantula fell down upon the bed, and in the hurry to find him, the plate of fat was upset, and all was pitch dark for a moment. As an additional comforter to us, one of the soldiers in the adjoining room cried out, 'Ah! there's a good many tarantu*lopes* in that 'ere room.'

So, what with the fleas, bugs, and the aforesaid *tarantulopes* and the noise of two entire horses, who were fighting and kicking one another all night, loose in the paddock, we had not a wink of sleep, and were glad to jump out of our dungeons at the first peep of day. The horses however, did not seem so glad to move as we did; a few quarts of corn, without grass or straw, does not do for a mountain journey; but it was only eighteen miles to the weather-boarded hut, where they would get another feed, and we intended to get breakfast.

The morning was cool and cloudy—threatening rain—the road in many places very good, and in other places very bad; we were already in a different climate, and still ascending as we proceeded. It was easy to see the difficulties which had impeded the first party who had penetrated across the range, although to us it was comparatively straight and pleasant. Near the sixteen mile tree, for the trees are marked all the way to Bathurst, is the spot where some years ago a gentleman of the name of O'Brien lost himself. It is supposed he left the ridge for the purpose of obtaining water for himself or horse, and going into the dell, met with some accident, and died, as he has never since been heard of. The horse was found some weeks afterwards, grazing on the mountain road with his saddle on. It is a melancholy spot—'all the evils of dereliction rush upon the thoughts'. We imagine the dying unfortunate,

> *Far from the track and blest abode of man;*
> *While round him, night, resistless, closes fast,*
> *And every tempest howling o'er his head,*
> *Renders the savage wilderness more wild.*

We now came to the ultima thule of Mr. Caley, the botanist, where the heap of stones was left when he attempted to cross the mountains, and which has ever since been known by the name of 'Caley's Repulse.' The road is now in this spot remarkably good; and at a place called the twenty mile hollow, which was the place that offered such insuperable difficulties to Mr. Caley, the road is now made by the prisoner gangs as good as the most capricious taste could desire. The traveller will here find a pretty spring of excellent water; and, as it is the first handy place for twenty miles, he should halt and take a drink.

The vegetation here becomes more dwarfish, and the tall ironbark trees of Springwood are now changed for stunted eucalyptus of box and ash, and several varieties of the honey-suckle (*Banksia integrifolia*), and now and then the telopea or waratah. We had determined to see the cataract of Bougainvill, as some have called it, since the visit of that navigator, but usually known by its first name of Campbell's Cataract. It lies about two miles off the road, at the Kings Tableland, which is nearly the highest point of the mountains, and for this reason can never, in the wettest weather, exhibit any large stream of water. We had some difficulty in getting down to the spot, and when there found the place enveloped in one thick fog, from the fretting stream, which would seem, for the most part, to be converted into vapour as it falls. To call it a cataract is absurd; it would be easy to make as good a one with a tea-kettle; but the abyss is awful, into which the little stream falls down, and had it been called the buller of the Blue Mountains (Bouilloire) for it is an immense cauldron, or chasm of unknown depth, perhaps two thousand feet perpendicular, the name would have been more appropriate. But name or no name, it is a remarkable spot, such as a visitor will never forget, and will amply repay the trouble and wetting of going out of the road. We scrambled down to the green point, as the mist drove past us; and, as soon as it became clearer, one of our party fired three rounds from his double barrelled gun, and with three cheers for the King, and a mouthful of mountain dew to drink his health, we returned to our horses, wet and black with the mossy grounds and burnt scrubs. The weather-boarded hut was only two miles further, and there we refreshed, at the highest inhabited spot of the Blue Mountains. It is a bleak and forbidding place, at the entrance of Jamison Valley; the soil is a wet and rotten peat, that after the least shower will take a horse up to the girths at every step. In addition to the [soldiers] stationed in this sterile region, we were surprised at finding an opposition shop newly opened, for the entertainment of travellers. What will not the spirit of English competition bring about! Here we were in one of the wildest spots in nature, thirty miles in the midst of the mountains; and yet the question arose, 'Which house shall we go to?' We patronised the nearest, and found ourselves and horses, after a couple of hours, all the better for the rest. Through Jamison Valley to Pulpit Hill, across Blackheath to the top of Mount York, the road is very good. Pitt's Amphitheatre, on the left, presents a noble tier of precipices, of bassalic appearance, and of unknown depths below. All was vast and wild, and dreary—fit for a poet:

> Welcome, ye everlasting hills!
> Temples of God; not made with hands!

The rain kept off, although not a gleam of sunshine had visited us the whole day. Here and there on the road side, we had seen the carcasses of bullocks that had died of starvation or fatigue across the mountain—sights which in the low country would have startled the mettle of our horses, but which they now looked upon without affright.

The descent down Mount York did not surprise me, after so much that has been said about it. It was the new road and comparatively easy. It is perfectly safe, but rather too narrow, as it will soon become cut up by water channels after a winter's rain. It should be at least twice the present breadth, with a deep grooved gutter on the high side for the water, and a low parapet on the off-side, of solid stone work, with numerous holes underneath, like scuppers in a ship's deck, to let the water off. We soon arrived at the bottom, where the ground was strewn with fallen trees, in great numbers, all regularly arranged by the road side. As the country was by no means thinly timbered, I could not conceive what these trees were intended for. They all appeared more or less black by age; and it was only after my companions had rode up from the rear that I understood how the trees came there. They put me in mind of the black stones at the foot of the hill in one of the Arabian tales, which, when sprinkled with a drop of the golden water, started up into horses and men. It appears that all carts coming down the Big Hill as this is called, must, ere they descend, cut down a tree at the top, to fix behind the dray, instead of locking the wheel. They were all of great weight and size, and I should have thought much too large for such a purpose. We were now in the Vale of Clwydd—a pretty, grassy plain, of small extent, hemmed in on every side but one, with lofty mountains, and after a smart ride of two miles, along the valley, we arrived at Collett's Inn, the Golden Fleece, the *'rest and be thankful'* of the Blue Mountains. We cannot pause at a better place …

I don't like the man who will travel from Dan to Beersheba, and tell us nothing. In a country like New South Wales, this disposition is particularly to be regretted, because every thing is new, even to the high road; and what little knowledge we may acquire of our common country, should, in my opinion, be thrown into the general fund. That old gentlemanly vice, avarice, that last infirmity of man, is bad enough, when merely confined to cash, but an avarice of knowledge is hateful and injurious. But all our knowledge of this fine country is little, and might be put in a nut-shell; and when we come to think of the interior, we know no more of it than we do of the moon! 'We are perfectly astonished,' said the officers of the French squadron, when they lay in Port Jackson a year ago, 'at your superb country.' 'What,' replied a gentleman, 'is it that most excites your surprise?' 'That you have been so long in it, and know so little about it,' was the severe answer. It was a just reproof, and ought to sink deep into the minds of those, who, by offering rewards of a few thousand acres of land, would set alive the spirit of discovery

—draw the whole eyes of Europe to our shores—redeem the character of our country men from the reproach of the French-men—and by thus fostering a laudable enterprise, secure to themselves an imperishable name! But it is no use talking—nothing will be done on a grand scale, the government hands are too full of business. Like the repentance of sailors in a storm,

> They vow to amend their lives and yet they don't,
> Because if drowned they can't—if saved they won't.

Collett's Inn is, I am sorry to say, only half-way to Bathurst, and bad as the preceding half was, the latter part of the jour-ney is the worst. The Vale of Clwydd reminds one of the valley of Bastan, in the pass of Ronscesvalles. But we must not forget mine host of the Golden Fleece and give him the go by in this way. I assure you there is only one better inn in the whole colony, for it is warm, comfortable, and commo-dious in the inside, as it is beautiful and picturesque without. The house is neat in the extreme, and the brightness, order and almost Dutch cleanliness of the kitchen pleased and sur-prised me. To arrive at Collett's is like passengers going a-shore from a weary voyage, everything appears à couleur de rose. There was just light enough the evening we got in, to see to shave and make ourselves comfortable after the filthy night at Springwood. Our horses were delivered over to the hostler, with perfect confidence that they would each get a belly full, for we were in a land of plenty; there was no neces-sity to stand by, stroking their tails, as somebody recommended in another place, while they devoured their thimble full of maize; their chafed backs were well bathed in salt and water, and we adjourned to the house, and discussed a supper in the midst of the Blue Mountains as good as we could have had, for aught I know, at the Blue Boar in Holborn. It was an American sort of supper, including excellent byson tea, dou-ble refined sugar, plenty of cream and butter, as hard as cheese, and the water crystal itself. When I saw such a plenty of good furniture, glass and earthenware, I at first wondered how such fragile furniture could have been brought so safely across the mountains, but felt no surprise as soon as I heard that the lime itself of which the house was built was brought all the way from Parramatta, a distance of seventy miles; and of course when they can bring lime, they may as well bring loaf sugar ...

The Fish River Hill is the worst hill from Sydney to Bathurst. We began to ascend immediately we left the ford; and never having been at Bathurst before, I could not help saying to myself, 'This Bathurst ought to be a fine place to come all this dreadful way to see it!' The sight of a four-rail fence, in Sidmouth Valley, after this weary hill, was the first symptom of humanity, for nearly ninety miles, and gave me unfeigned pleasure. We had now passed the Blue Mountains, and were in a tolerable country—thinly timbered, but hilly—affording good pasture on the high grounds for sheep, and presenting in the valley a vegetable mould, ten or twelve feet deep, as black as jet, resting on yellow ochre, dry and friable, containing mica and iron pyrites. A crop of excellent wheat had not long been off the ground and it was pleasing to see this first settler, upwards of eighty miles from Emu Plains, with a beautiful new cottage and substantial barns, outhouses, fencing &c. The adjoining farm, of four thousand acres, is the property of a respectable merchant in Sydney, and has a very large commodious cottage on it, with good out-buildings &c. The country now improves every mile, and seven or eight miles on this side of Bathurst Plains you might suppose yourself once more in Leon or Estremadura. Downs would give you a better idea of this country in the neighbourhood of Bathurst, than the word plains. There is said to be thirty thousand acres of this open exposed country upon which there is not a tree or shrub as high as the candle by which I am writing. It is far, however, from being a plain country, as it rises in numerous swelling hills, of a dry siliceous earth, by no means deep, bearing a sweet but scanty grass, which at this hot season of the year, and after an unusual drought, was a good deal burnt up. The farms of the Messrs. Lawson, Cox and Hassal appeared all to great advantage, and with those of Messrs. Street, Mackenzie and West, are calculated to impress the visitor with a very favourable opinion of Bathurst. If a man could be put down here in a balloon, or find some royal road to the country, without having anything to do with the Blue Mountains, he would hug himself with a constant satisfaction, and desire to know no more …

The greatest number of respectable settlers are found in this direction. On the left of the road are a number of small thirty and fifty acre farms, belonging to small settlers, formerly prisoners, whose white-washed houses and glazed windows, good gardens, and golden coloured stacks of wheat indicate a degree of industry and ease that was pleasing to contemplate. The river Macquarie ran close to us, at the bottom of these little farms, broad, clear and rapid, and excited the most lively sensations, like the Niger of Africa, by reason of its unknown course. The fatigues of the journey were now over, and we were really in a Christian country—the climate mild and delightful—the prospect cheerful and extensive— the sheep returning to the fold seemed healthy and happy, and awakened thoughts of abundance—of content—of thankfulness. The gorgeous sun was setting in a robe of gold, over that undiscovered country west of the Macquarie, and the scene was altogether worthy of a Claude.

Here finishes, at this celebrated river, this modern Jordan, the fine property of the settlers; all beyond is the Government's! which has hitherto been considered too good to give away. 'You may look at the heavenly country, but touch not! taste not! handle not!' has been, till the present moment, the tenor of all the General Orders upon this subject. The settlement or *city* is on the Government side of the river; and is the most paltry, contemptible thing imaginable. 'Where's Bathurst?' I frequently enquired, and when we crossed the ford, where so many men have been *drowned for the want of a bridge*, and was told 'this is Bathurst,' I positively burst out laughing. Is the Majesty of Great Britain reduced to this? … the mere spot properly called Bathurst, or the settlement, being the wretchedest place in New South Wales, whereas if given out in allotments to settlers, it might soon become one of the finest.

In justice to the present government, however, it must be admitted, that the supreme folly of these overgrown government establishments, *in the heart of the settlers*, is not to be laid at their door. The system was a favourite one with Macquarie, and has extended its withering influence, like the Sirocco, all the way from the coast to this western country ...

I have told you before, and I now tell you again, that for so limited a population, there is not a shrewder or a richer people in the world than the people of New South Wales— more enthusiastically fond of the liberty and institutions of their fatherland; and where the foundations are being laid, quietly but certainly, of such numerous and princely fortunes from the growth of wool. Like Madeira wine, the voyage tends to improve all emigrants to this country, added to which, when here, you find so many men cleverer than yourself, that the mind is compelled to reflection, and we are glad to ask advice ... The settlers at Bathurst are all doing well, notwithstanding the disadvantages of their great distance, and mountain road. How can it be otherwise in a country so peculiarly adapted to the growth of fine wool as New South Wales ...

We saw very few native blacks, only three, in a ride of four hundred miles. Those were stout athletic fellows, clothed in large cloaks of opossum skin, neatly sewed together, and whose beards were eight or nine inches long, as though they had been Turks. The black race is visibly declining in numerical strength every year ... For want of white female companions the distant stock-keepers are eaten up with disease, the results of their connection with the black women. The contagion is going through the natives with the most fatal ravages, and will gradually put an end to them, more certainly than sword or musket ...

A most important piece of news has been lately communicated by a party of black fellows to our stockmen at Wellington Valley, which, if true, may hereafter materially effect our commercial and agricultural interests across the mountains. The tribes who occupy the country two and three days journey from Wellington Valley have been engaged in war several years with the tribes living further west and north-west; but owing to the death of one of the chiefs, peace has been at length restored between them, and these *mial* or strange blacks have related to their new friends, and these to us, that there exists in the western country, many days off, a vast interior sea, where the water is salt, and where whales are seen to spout! The manner in which they imitated the whale throwing up water was so completely satisfactory as to leave little doubt of the fact, and it is not likely these inland blacks could have known it but from actual observation.

X.Y.Z.

VII

James Blackhouse

The Quaker's story

J ames Blackhouse and another British Quaker comprised the first religious mission the Society of Friends sent to Australia. As this account of their crossing the mountains in both directions in 1835 indicates, their interest in religion was not always shared by the people they found themselves among.

———

9th mo. lst. Having made application for leave to visit the prisoners, in the jails, penitentiaries, ironed-gangs &c., in the colony, we received a document today, signed by the Colonial Secretary, on behalf of the Governor, granting us this permission …

2nd. We went to Parramatta, by a steamer, and took up our quarters at a respectable inn. This town is the second in size in New South Wales. In the census taken in 1833, it contained 2,637 inhabitants. Its population, at this time, will probably be about four thousand.

3rd. We breakfasted with Samuel Marsden and his family, at the parsonage. After breakfast, he drove us to the Female Factory, and the Female Orphan School. The former is a large stone building, enclosed within a wall sixteen feet high, divided into a number of wards, and having distinct yards, for assignable prisoners, and for those under sentence. There are sixteen solitary cells, in all of which prisoners were suffering punishment, chiefly for drunkenness and insolence.

The number of females sentenced to confinement in this factory, exclusive of those assignable, is about 250; who, it is to be regretted, are nearly destitute of employment. Formerly, women of this character were employed in spinning, and in weaving coarse, woollen cloth, but this occupation has been abandoned. The rooms where it was carried on are empty, and like those of other parts of the building, have the glass of the windows much broken. This is said to have been done by some of the women, in unruly fits, which they occasionally take, one exciting another. This is not to be wondered at, among so large a number of the worst portion of the females of Great Britain and Ireland, confined but unemployed. The assignable women were occupied with needlework, and the place they were in was clean. The Female Orphan School is a good brick building, kept neat and clean; it contains 150 children, who are generally healthy, and much like others of the same age.

On returning from the Orphan School, we called upon the Governor, and at his request, accompanied him to inspect the site of a projected lunatic asylum, at Tarban Creek … [between Hunters Hill and Huntleys Point].

6th. Having believed it our duty to invite the inhabitants to a religious meeting, we engaged a large room belonging to the inn, where only a small company assembled this morning. We had but little to express among them; that little was, however, illustrative of the nature of true worship; and access was granted to the throne of Grace, in prayer, near the conclusion. Another meeting, held in the evening, was larger. The overshadowing of the divine presence was more perceptibly felt and the doctrines of the Gospel were more largely preached than in the former. After the state of the country, from drought, had been noticed, and the passage, 'He turneth a fruitful land into barrenness, for the wickedness of them that dwell therein' and some others relating to such dispensations of the Almighty had been commented upon, the benefits of silence before the Lord were also spoken of, and prayer was vocally offered; after which, a solemn pause concluded the meeting.

7th. Samuel Marsden provided us with a guide to south creek: he was a black, of that place, named Johnny, an intelligent man, speaking English very fairly, and wearing a hat, jacket, trousers and shoes. He carried our bundles and was very attentive, and by no means meriting the character given to us this morning, of their race, by a settler from Wollongong: 'That nothing could be given to these fellows that they valued a straw.' I could not think the person who made the remark had attained to much knowledge of human nature. It is quite true that the blacks have not learned to place the same value upon many things that the whites place upon them. It is amusing to see the disappointment of many of the whites at the proofs they meet with of this fact, especially when they think to hold out temptations to the blacks to work for less than their labour is worth. Few white people seem to reflect upon the fact that our notions of the value of things depend upon our habits, and are, in many instances, merely ideal. It is, however, to be regretted when benevolent men adopt the notion that the circumstances of the blacks not estimating things by the same standard as the whites, is owing to some invincible peculiarity in them, because such an opinion paralyzes their efforts for the civilization of this untutored race.

On the way from Parramatta we stepped into several cottages, conversed with the inhabitants, and gave them tracts. We had also many conversations with persons travelling on the road on foot, in carts, &c. We were kindly received by Charles Marsden [brother of Samuel] and his family, at the

south creek, sixteen miles from Parramatta, and in the evening
had a satisfactory religious interview with them and their
servants. Before dark, we walked to the side of the creek to
see the black natives, who resort thither. In comparison with
some other tribes, the south creek natives may be considered
as half-domesticated, and they often assist in the agricultural
operations of the settlers. The wife of our guide can read, she
is a half-caste, who was educated in a school formerly kept for
the natives at Parramatta. It is to be regretted that this school
was abandoned; for though many who were educated in it
returned into the woods, yet an impression was made upon
them favourable to their further progress in civilization.

A few of the natives were at one time located upon a
piece of the worst land in this part of the country, at a place
called Black Town. Here some of them raised grain, in spite
of the sterility of the soil, at a time when they were unable to
dispose of it; and, to add to their discouragement, at this
juncture the missionary who had been a short time among
them was withdrawn. The want of success in this unfair ex-
periment is sometimes brought forward as a proof that nothing can be done for these injured and neglected people.

8th. We set out at an early hour to Penrith, a small, scattered
town on the Nepean River. Our guide was another south
creek black, named Simeon. His wife was killed about two
years ago by some of those whom he termed 'Wild natives'.
He had one little boy, for whom he showed great affection.
We tried in vain to persuade this man to accompany us to
Wellington Valley; he did not like to go to so great a distance.
These people are afraid of other tribes of their own race ...

After travelling eighteen miles, we arrived at the
Weather-board Hut where we had intended to lodge, but
the only good room was occupied. One in which we had an
excellent meal of beef and bread, with tea, was without glass
in the windows, and could not have the door shut, for the
smoking of the wood fire. This , as is common in this land of
trees, was a very large one, and it was acted upon by a fierce
and piercing wind; we therefore determined on making

another stage. The former part of our journey through the forest had been cheered, at intervals, by remarkable views. Some of these opened to a great distance, exhibiting the singularly winding cliffs of sandstone, which seemed as if it had decomposed, till ferruginous veins had bid defiance to the weather. We now set out again, as daylight was departing, to make our way in the dark. We were informed that there was but one road through the woods, yet we sometimes felt a little perplexed by this road dividing for a short distance. But notwithstanding these difficulties, we found our previously exhausted vigour to increase as we proceeded, in consequence of the bracing effects of the cold wind; and we reached the 'Scotch Thistle', a solitary inn, at Black Heath, on top of the mountains, earlier than we expected.

The road over the Blue Mountains winds nearly forty miles along their ridge, which ascends and descends a little at intervals. Some parts of it have been cut with much labour, by prisoners, and others are sandy or rocky, but most of it is now good for carriages. There are a few miserable, solitary public-houses by its side, in addition to the better ones already mentioned, and another of decent character. Along its whole course there are no grassy openings to afford pasturage for cattle. At the present time the little rigid herbage, in the forest, is dried up. The bullocks travelling with the settlers' drays, are 'ill favoured and lean fleshed', from the scarcity of grass in the countries below. Dead bullocks were numerous by the road side. Wedge-tailed Eagles were frequently to be seen, feeding upon the fresh ones …

11th. Last evening, we had a religious interview with the family, and a few other persons, who had called to beg a night's lodging. This morning, one of our young friends accompanied us over some of the grassy, forest hills, to the road leading to the Junction Stockade, where an ironed-gang, of upwards of 150 prisoners, is employed, under the charge of a military officer. These men were at work, cutting a road, about three miles from the barracks, under a guard of soldiers, some of whom returned from Norfolk Island in the *Isabella* at the same time with ourselves. We assembled the men by the road-side, and extended some religious counsel to them; the guard standing at the time, as they generally do, in a position to prevent any of the prisoners running away. The soldiers often use irritating language, mixed with curses, in speaking to the prisoners, which is of bad influence, in hardening them, when they greatly need to be rendered more susceptible of good. While in the act of assembling, one man picked the pocket of another, of a tobacco-box: he was seen, and knocked down by one of the guard, near to the place where I was standing. The circumstances occasioned no perceptible disturbance among the others, and I trust there were some present who, at least, for the time, were brought to think on eternal things.

Near the barracks we saluted a native black and his wife, and they returned our tokens of notice. They were the first we had seen in their wild state. We took some refreshment at a decent public-house, at Solitary Creek, and afterwards visited a small road-party, on the way to an inn, at Honeysuckle Hill. As we approached this place in the dark we heard the cries of a female, and on arriving found that the landlord, in a state of intoxication, had struck his wife to the ground, with a child in her arms; and such was his frenzy that it was difficult to restrain him from further mischief.

12th. We visited a small road-party near the foot of the Stony Ridge, and another betwixt that place and Bathurst. It was past their work-hours, on seventh-day afternoon, before we reached the last party, and several of the men pleaded that they were Roman Catholics, and did not wish to come to 'prayers' as they style all kinds of religious interviews. With some difficulty we got them to understand our object, and most of them assembled in a rude blacksmith's shop, in which we were glad of a shelter from the cold. The message of love and mercy made a softening impression upon these prisoners, and we separated under different feelings, on their part, from those with which they met us. This we find generally the case. The baptizing power of the Holy Spirit is felt, and their attention turned to their own convictions of sin, as the work of this blessed Spirit, and as the message of their Heavenly Father, seeking to lead them to repentance, in order that they may obtain salvation through his beloved Son.

When we stop them during their work-hours, which we have liberty from the Governor to do, few plead excuses; and as we do not enjoin any forms of worship, but simply, after a pause, say what is upon our minds, or pray for them, none seem to take it amiss. If it can be done, we always desire them to sit down, in order that they may rest at the same time; and if exposed to the sun, we request them to keep on their hats or caps. These little considerations for their personal comfort often prepare the way for the reception of our counsel ...

While at Bathurst I saw much drunkenness, such as is common in remote situations in these colonies. Many men, and some women, who appeared to be servants of settlers, were drinking at public-houses. It is common with the men, many of whom have been prisoners but have served out their sentence, to engage themselves as sawyers, shepherds, &c., in distant places, and to come into town, when they have earned a few pounds, for the sole purpose of spending it in drunkenness and debauchery. When their money is gone they return again to their labour. But for this, many of them might have been in easy circumstances, for they get good wages, and a little sets a man up in this part of the world. They prove the truth of the proverb, 'The workman that is a drunkard will never be rich.' ...

Having concluded our labours at Bathurst, we accompanied a respectable settler, residing at Woodlands, at the junction of the Campbell and Fish Rivers, to his comfortable residence.

10th. The country about Woodlands is fine; the soil is a mixture of decomposed basaltic and granitic rocks, with pieces of rolled Jasper scattered on the surface. In a well of seventy feet deep, in which water has not yet been obtained, a substance resembling soap-stone occurs, under the decomposed granite. Several of the neighbouring settlers dined with us. Considering the shortness of the time since the Blue Mountains were first crossed by Europeans, the respectability of the population in this district is remarkable. They are placed under inconvenience at present by the difficulties of obtaining necessaries, from the long drought, which has weakened the cattle, and has caused the expense of carriage over the mountains, to be very great ...

13th. Our route lay along the Fish River, which here has a granite bed, and except in rainy weather, is a slender stream. It takes its name from a fish, about the size of a Cod, that inhabits its waters. We passed over a ridge of granite and compact sandstone, the highest point of which is called Evans' Crown. *Exarrhena suaveolens*, a plant resembling Forget-me-not, but having large, white, fragrant flowers, and some others, common also in Van Diemen's Land but rare in New South Wales, were growing here. The mid-way sun was very hot, and snakes, basking in its rays, were numerous. Two young dogs belonging to one of our friends from Helvellyn, who accompanied us from O'Connell Plains, killed four. One of the dogs barked in front of the snake, while the other seized it in its mouth, gave it a violent shake, and dropped it. The other then barked, while his fellow attacked the reptile. This they continued, at the risk of their lives, till one of our party finished the destruction of the snakes with a stick. At Antonios Creek we were refreshed with milk and damper, by a man formerly a prisoner. Milk is now so plentiful at many stations that, where they have not pigs to consume it, much of it is thrown away after the cream is taken off.

14th. One of the prisoners at the house where we lodged, having been flogged by order of a magistrate for allowing the sheep to ramble over a piece of marshy ground, the whole of those at the establishment refused to come to the reading of the Scriptures last evening. I went to them this morning and gave them some counsel, which was well received.

We pursued our way to Black Heath. The advance of spring has decorated the Vale of Clywdd, as well as the Blue Mountains, with many pretty blossoms. Among these may be enumerated several species of *Grevillea*, a genus, including shrubs, with handsome flowers but of very various foliage, aspect, and altitude; some of them are creepers on the ground, others are lofty trees.

Arriving at Black Heath early, and not thinking it prudent to proceed further today, we turned aside to visit Govett's Leap, where at an interval of a few hundred yards, two small streams fall over a precipice, at the opposite sides of a cove, in a sandstone cliff. The cove is half a mile or more in width, extending beyond the falls, and having ledges upon which shrubs are growing, notwithstanding that to the eye it appears perpendicular. The perpendicular fall of one of the streams is calculated at six hundred feet. The water is diffused into a shower of drops before it reaches a mound of moss that has grown up from below to meet it. The other fall is somewhat less in height. The course of the water from the foot of the cliff is traceable, in the dense forest of 'the inaccessible valley', where it joins the Grose River, by the darker verdure and the tree-ferns on the margins of the streams. The cliffs, on the opposite side of this dark glen are of similar character, forming a long series of coves. Above them rise some considerably woody eminences, on which the snow lies in winter …

15th. We set out in a smart snow storm, dined at the Weatherboard-hut [Wentworth Falls], and reached the valley in the evening. Several showers of hail and rain fell in the course of the day. In the lower altitudes of the mountains, the advance of spring was more striking. *Telopea speciosissima*, forming low bushes, with heads of flowers as large as small Peonies, was in full blossom. The Blue Mountain Parrot, partly blue, and with a breast of crimson as brilliant as the flowers, was drinking nectar out of the blossoms of this splendid shrub; and a brown Honey-eater was darting its tongue, like a slender pencil of hair, into the elegant pink flowers of *Grevillea*

linearis. Gompholobium grandiflorium, a large yellow, pea-flow-
ered shrub of great beauty, and several species of *Platylobium*,
Daviesia, *Boronia* and *Eriostemon*, enlivened the solitude and
beguiled the walk of thirty-one miles through this dreary
forest, which we accomplished in ten hours. This kind of
exercise, in such a climate, gives vigour to the digestive pow-
ers and cheerfulness to the spirits. The number of dead bullocks had increased considerably since we last crossed the
mountains. We fell in with several parties of men with drays,
conveying supplies for the settlers to the westward. Some of
them were resting, others pursuing their way with cattle, so
weak that many of them appeared likely to die before reaching the other side. Notwithstanding the late rains have caused
the grass again to grow, it is still very scarce in the little mountain glens, where it is not of a nutritious quality; and the
cattle in the low countries have not yet had time, since the
rain fell, to get into such condition as is necessary to enable
them to endure such a journey.

16th. Toward the close of the day we overtook a magistrate,
returning from an inquest on the remains of a woman who
had hung herself, in a state of excitement from drinking. Her
husband had been committed to prison on the charge of wilful
murder, for having assisted his wife in the accomplishment of
this rash and wicked act! The man was afterwards tried, found
guilty, and sentenced to death; but was respited till the opinion of the English judges could be had, upon the before un-
heard of case; and this opinion had not been received when I
left New South Wales ...

On visiting the police office at Penrith to apply for
leave to hold a meeting in it, we witnessed the infliction of
the degrading punishment of flagellation on two prisoners,
to the amount of one hundred lashes each. One of them bore
his punishment without complaint; the other writhed much
under it, complained piteously, and was so faint as to require
to be frequently supplied with water. Yet I saw this man, a
few minutes after, putting on his clothes behind the jail, and
jeering with a woman, in a way that proved that his mind was

not beneficially operated upon, though in body he must have suffered severely, unless the torpor of the mutilated flesh rendered him temporarily insensible. I believe the disposition of mind of those who think to keep mankind in subjection by severity is much the same as it was in Rehoboam, when he took the counsel of the young men; and that it will, in one way or other, lead to similar results ...

At Penrith a Jew, professing Christianity, the father-in-law of the landlord of the inn, told us that, as we had come among them to preach the gospel, we should be free of all charges. We acknowledged his kindness, and explained how our expenses were paid, to which he replied, he hoped we would not debar him of this privilege.

18th. At ten o'clock a small congregation met us at the police office at Penrith, where religion and morality are at a low ebb. In the afternoon we had a meeting at Nepean, which was well attended. The Wesleyans preach here occasionally, but the tone of religious feeling is low ...

After meeting we called to see an aged man, who had been confined to bed with palsy for several years, and was in a state of great suffering. He was formerly a prisoner, became thoughtful without instrumental means, got a little forward in his circumstances, gave the land where the school-house is built, and reared a large family, by some of whom he has been in danger of being again led away from righteousness, by their joining a medical man in recommending him to take spirits as a medicine ...

23rd. We went to Richmond, another little town on the Hawkesbury, four miles distant from Windsor. The country here is very fine and productive, with extensive grassy flats along the sides of the river. On these, people continue to build and reside, notwithstanding there have been floods, at intervals of a few years, that have risen far above the tops of their houses.

A respectable Wesleyan at Richmond told us that he had heard of our visit to Wellington Valley, several days ago,

from a native, who had had the particulars detailed to him by
a black from that country. Our persons, costume, and many
other particulars, including our manner of communicating
religious instruction, had been minutely described. And our
Wesleyan friend inquiring what the black supposed all this to
mean, he replied, 'God Almighty come and sit down at Wellington'; implying that the Most High would be worshipped
there. The scattered natives of Australia communicate information rapidly; messengers being often sent from tribe to
tribe for great distances. In the evening we returned to Windsor.

24th. Accompanied by a thoughtful military officer, we walked to the villages of Pitt Town and Wilberforce. At Pitt Town
we were helped, in obtaining a place to hold a meeting in, by
the Episcopal Minister.

25th. We had meetings at Richmond in the forenoon, and at
Windsor in the afternoon.

26th. We had some conversation with an unfaithful professor
of religion, with whom we expostulated, on his inconsist-
ency, in endeavouring to add to his income by distilling
spirits, both to his own injury and to that of those who
consumed them. This man tried to vindicate his practice, but
himself became gradually ensnared by the insidious poison;
he ultimately died of delirium tremens. We also visited some
thoughtful people, not professing with any associated body
of Christians; one of whom left the army on half-pay, when
he became religiously awakened, finding military associations
inimical to his religious progress.

In the evening a temperance meeting was held in the
government school-room, when we gave the company some
information on the progress of temperance societies. There
are about ninety members here, many of whom are soldiers:
one of their officers is a diligent labourer in this good cause.

VIII

Charles Darwin

Two distinct creators

In 1836 Darwin landed at Sydney as part of his five-year trip around the world in the *Beagle*. It was during this journey that he collected much of the information that went to forming the theory of evolution. Some readers have suggested that the lion-ant observation in the following excerpt contains one of the seeds from which the theory was to grow.

Darwin's journal of his journey was published soon after his return to England, and became a very popular travel book.

I hired a man and two horses to take me to Bathurst; a village about one hundred and twenty miles in the interior, and the centre of a great pastoral district. By this means I hoped to get a general idea of the appearance of the country. On the morning of the 16th [January] I set out on my excursion. The first stage took us to Parramatta, a small country-town, the second to Sydney in importance. The roads were excellent, and made upon the MacAdam principle: whinstone having been brought for the purpose from the distance of several miles. The road appeared much frequented by all sorts of carriages; and I met two stage-coaches. In all these respects there was a close resemblance to England; perhaps the number of alehouses was here in excess. The iron gangs, or parties of convicts, who have here committed some trifling offence, appeared the least like England; they were working in chains, under the charge of sentries with loaded arms. The power, which the government possesses, by means of forced labour, of at once opening good roads throughout the country, has been, I believe, one main cause of the early prosperity of this colony.

I slept at night at a very comfortable inn at Emu ferry, thirty-five miles from Sydney, and near the ascent of the Blue Mountains. This line of road is the most frequented, and has been the longest inhabited of any in the colony. The whole land is enclosed with high railings, for the farmers have not succeeded in rearing hedges. There are many substantial houses and good cottages scattered about; but although considerable pieces of land are under cultivation, the greater part yet remains as when first discovered. Making allowances for the cleared parts, the country here resembled all that I saw during the ten succeeding days.

The extreme uniformity of the vegetation is the most remarkable feature in the landscape of the greater part of New South Wales. Everywhere we have an open woodland; the ground being partially covered with a very thin pasture. The trees nearly all belong to one family; and mostly have the surface of their leaves placed in a vertical, instead of as in Europe, a nearly horizontal position; the foliage is scanty, and of a peculiar, pale green tint, without any gloss. Hence the woods appear light and shadowless: this, although a loss of comfort to the traveller under the scorching rays of summer, is of importance to the farmer, as it allows grass to grow where it otherwise could not. The leaves are not shed periodically: this character appears common to the entire southern hemisphere, namely south America, Australia, and the Cape of Good Hope. The inhabitants of this hemisphere and of the intertropical regions thus lose perhaps one of the most glorious, though to our eyes common, spectacles in the world—the first bursting into full foliage of the leafless tree. They may, however, say that we pay dearly for our spectacle, by having the land covered with mere naked skeletons for so many months. This is too true; but our senses thus acquire a keen relish for the exquisite green of the spring, which the eyes of those living within the tropics, sated during the long year with the gorgeous productions of those glowing climates, can never experience. The greater number of the trees, with the exception of some of the blue gums, do not attain a large size; but they grow tall and tolerably straight, and stand well apart. The bark of some falls annually, or hangs dead in long shreds, which swing about with the wind; and hence the woods appear desolate and untidy. Nowhere is there an appearance of verdure, but rather that of arid sterility. I cannot imagine a more complete contrast in every respect than between the forests of Valdiva, or Chiloe, in Chile, and the woods of Australia.

Although this colony flourishes so remarkably, the appearance of infertility is to a certain degree real. The soil without doubt is good, but there is so great a deficiency both of rain and running water, that it cannot produce much. The agricultural crops, and often those in gardens, are estimated to fail once in three years; and this has even happened on successive years. Hence the colony cannot supply itself with the bread and vegetables which its inhabitants consume. It is essentially pastoral, and chiefly so for sheep, and not the larger quadrupeds. The alluvial land near Emu ferry was some of the best cultivated which I saw; and certainly the scenery on the banks of the Nepean, bounded to the west by the Blue Mountains, was pleasing even to the eye of a person thinking of England.

At sunset, a party of a score of the black Aborigines passed by, each carrying, in their accustomed manner, a bundle of spears and other weapons. By giving a leading young man a shilling, they were easily detained, and threw their spears for my amusement. They were all partly clothed, and several could speak a little English; their countenances were good humoured and pleasant; and they appeared far from being such utterly degraded beings as they are usually represented. In their own arts they are admirable: a cap being fixed at thirty yards distance, they transfixed it with a spear, delivered by the throwing stick, with the rapidity of an arrow from the bow of a practised archer. In tracking animals or men they show most wonderful sagacity, and I heard of several of their remarks which manifested considerable acuteness. They will not, however, cultivate the ground, or build houses and remain stationary, or even take the trouble of tending a flock of sheep when given to them. On the whole they appear to me to stand some few degrees higher in the scale of civilization than the Fuegians.

It is very curious thus to see in the midst of a civilized people, a set of harmless savages wandering about without knowing where they shall sleep at night, and gaining their livelihood by hunting in the woods. As the white man has travelled onwards, he has spread over the country belonging to several tribes. These, although thus enclosed by one common people, keep up their ancient distinctions, and sometimes go to war with each other. In an engagement which took place lately, the two parties most singularly chose the centre of the village of Bathurst for the field of battle. This was of service to the defeated side, for the runaway warriors took refuge in the barracks.

The number of Aborigines is rapidly decreasing. In my whole ride, with the exception of some boys brought up in the houses, I saw only one other party; these were rather more numerous than the first, and not so well clothed. This decrease, no doubt, must be partly owing to the introduction of spirits, to European diseases (even the milder ones of which, as the measles, prove very destructive), and to the gradual extinction of the wild animals. It is said that numbers of their children invariably perish in very early infancy from the effects of their wandering life. As the difficulty of procuring food increases, so must their wandering habits; and hence the population, without any apparent deaths from famine, is repressed in a manner extremely sudden compared to what happens in civilized countries, where the father may add to his labour without destroying his offspring.

Besides these several evident causes of destruction, there appears to be some more mysterious agency generally at work. Wherever the European has trod, death seems to pursue the aboriginal. We may look to the wide extent of the Americas, Polynesia, the Cape of Good Hope, and Australia, and we shall find the same result. Nor is it the white man alone that thus acts the destroyer; the Polynesian of Malay extraction has in parts of the east Indian archipelago thus driven before him the dark-coloured native. The varieties of man may seem to act on each other, in the same way as different species of animals—the stronger always exterminating the weaker. It was melancholy at New Zealand to hear the fine energetic natives saying they knew the land was doomed to pass from their children. Everyone has heard of the inexplicable reduction of the population in the beautiful and healthy island of Tahiti since the date of Captain Cook's voyages; although in that case we might have expected it would have been otherwise; for infanticide, which formerly prevailed to so extraordinary a degree, has ceased, and the murderous wars have become less frequent.

January 17. Early in the morning we passed the Nepean in a ferry-boat. The river, although at this spot both broad and deep, had a very small body of running water. Having crossed a low piece of land on the opposite side, we reached the slope of the Blue Mountains. The ascent is not steep, the road having been cut with much care on the side of a sandstone cliff. [A new route, designed by Surveyor-General Thomas Mitchell, had been opened in 1834.] At no great elevation an almost level plain extends, which, rising imperceptibly to the westward, at last attains a height of more than three thousand feet. From so grand a title as Blue Mountains, and from their absolute altitude, I expected to have seen a bold chain of mountains crossing the country; but instead of this, a sloping plain presents merely an inconsiderable front to the low land of the coast. From this first slope the view of the extensive woodland to the eastward was striking, and the surrounding trees grew bold and lofty. But when once on the sandstone platform, the scenery becomes exceedingly monotonous: each side of the road is bordered by scrubby trees of the never-failing Eucalyptus family; and with the exception of two or three small inns, there are no houses, or cultivated land; the road, moreover, is solitary; the most frequent object being a bullock-wagon, piled up with bales of wool.

In the middle of the day we baited our horses at a little inn, called the Weatherboard. The country here [at Wentworth Falls] is elevated 2,800 feet above the sea. About a mile and a half from this place there is a view exceedingly well worth visiting. By following down a little valley and its tiny rill of water, an immense gulf is unexpectedly seen through the trees, which border the pathway, at the depth of perhaps 1,500 feet. Walking on a few yards one stands on the brink of a vast precipice, and below is the grand bay or gulf (for I know not what other name to give it), thickly covered with forest. The point of view is situated as if at the head of a bay, the line of cliff diverging on each side, and showing headland behind headland, as on a bold sea-coast. These cliffs are composed of horizontal strata of whitish sandstone, and so absolutely vertical are they that in many places a person standing on the edge, and throwing down a stone, can see it strike the trees in the abyss below. So unbroken is the line that it is said, in order to reach the foot of the waterfall formed by this little stream, it is necessary to go a distance of sixteen miles round. About five miles distant in front, another line of cliffs extends, which thus appears completely to encircle the valley; and hence the name of bay is justified, as applied to this grand amphitheatrical depression. If we imagine a winding harbour, with its deep water surrounded by bold cliff-like shores, laid dry, and a forest sprung up on its sandy bottom, we should then have the appearance and structure here exhibited. This kind of view was to me quite novel, and extremely magnificent.

In the evening, we reached the blackheath. The sandstone plateau has here attained the elevation of 3,400 feet; and is covered, as before, with the same kind of scrubby wood. From the road there were occasional glimpses into a profound valley, of the same character as the one described; but from the steepness and depth of its sides, the bottom was scarcely ever to be seen. The Blackheath is a very comfortable inn, kept by an old soldier; and it reminded me of the small inns in north Wales. I was surprised to find that here, at the distance of more than seventy miles from Sydney, fifteen beds could be made up for travellers.

January 18. Very early in the morning, I walked about three miles to see Govett's Leap: a view of similar but even perhaps more stupendous character than that near the Weatherboard. So early in the day the gulf was filled with a thin blue haze, which, although destroying the general effect, added to the apparent depth at which the forest was stretched below the country on which we were standing. Soon after leaving the Blackheath, we descended from the sandstone platform by the pass of Mount Victoria. To effect this pass, an enormous quantity of stone has been cut through; the design, and its manner of execution, would have been worthy of any line of road in England, even that of Holyhead. [This was another of Mitchell's new routes, opened in 1832 and still in use today.] We now entered upon a country less elevated by nearly a thousand feet, and consisting of granite. With the change of rock, the vegetation improved; the trees were both finer, and stood further apart; and the pasture between them was a little greener, and more plentiful.

At Hassan's Walls I left the high road and made a short detour to a farm called Wallerawang, to the superintendent of which I had a letter of introduction from the owner in Sydney. Mr. Browne had the kindness to ask me to stay the ensuing day, which I had much pleasure in doing. This place offers an example of one of the large farming, or rather sheep-grazing, establishments of the colony. Cattle and horses are, however, in this case, rather more numerous than usual, owing to some of the valleys being swampy, and producing a coarser pasture. The sheep were 15,000 in number, of which the greater part were feeding under the care of different shepherds, on unoccupied ground, at the distance of more than a hundred miles, and beyond the limits of the colony. Mr. Browne had just finished, this day, the last of the shearing of seven thousand sheep; the rest being sheared in another place. I believe the profit of the average produce of wool from 15,000 sheep would be more than 5,000/- sterling. Two or three flat pieces of ground near the house were cleared and cultivated with corn, which the harvest men were now reaping, but no more wheat is sown than sufficient for the annual support of the labourers employed on the establishment. The usual number of assigned convict servants here is about forty, but at the present time there were rather more. Although the farm was well stocked with every requisite, there was an apparent lack of comfort; and not even a single woman resided here. The sunset of a fine day will generally cast an air of happy contentment on any scene; but here, at this retired farm-house, the brightest tints on the surrounding woods could not make me forget that forty hardened, profligate men, were ceasing from their daily labours, like the slaves from Africa, yet without their just claim for compassion.

Early on the next morning, Mr. Archer, the joint superintendent, had the kindness to take me out kangaroo-hunting. We continued riding for the greater part of the day, but had very bad sport, not seeing a kangaroo, or even a wild dog. The greyhounds pursued a kangaroo rat into a hollow tree, out of which we dragged it; it is an animal as big as a rabbit, but with the figure of a kangaroo. A few years since, this country abounded with wild animals; but now the emu is banished to a long distance, and the kangaroo is become scarce; to both, the English greyhound is utterly destructive. It may be long before these animals are altogether exterminated, but their doom is fixed. The natives are always anxious to borrow the dogs from the farmhouses: the use of them, the offal when an animal is killed, and milk from the cows, are the peace-offerings of the settlers, who push further and

Bridal Veil Falls, Govett's Leap

Wentworth Falls

Bark of Angophora costata

Mount Solitary and Mount Jamison Valley

Bank's Wall, Grose Valley

further towards the interior. The thoughtless aboriginal, blinded by these trifling advantages, is delighted at the approach of the white man, who seems predestined to inherit the country of his children.

Although having bad sport we enjoyed a pleasant ride. The woodland is generally so open that a person on horseback can gallop through it. It is traversed by a few flat-bottomed valleys, which are green and free from trees: in such spots the scenery was like that of a park, and pretty. In the whole country I scarcely saw a place without the marks of fire; whether these had been more or less recent—whether the stumps were more or less black, was the greatest change which varied the uniformity, so wearisome to the traveller's eye. In these woods there are not many birds; I saw, however, some large flocks of the white cockatoo feeding in a cornfield, and a few most beautiful parrots; crows like our jackdaws were not uncommon, and another bird something like the magpie. The English have not been very particular in giving names to the productions of Australia; trees of one genus (*Casuarina*) are called oaks for no one reason that I can discover, without it is that there is no one point of resemblance. Some quadrupeds are called tigers and hyenas, simply because they are carnivorous, and so on in many other cases.

In the dusk of the evening I took a stroll along a chain of ponds, which in this dry country represented the course of a river [the Cox's], and had the good fortune to see several of the famous Platypus, or *Ornithorhynchus paradoxus*. They were diving and playing about the surface of the water, but showed so little of their bodies that they might easily have been mistaken for water-rats. Mr. Browne shot one: certainly it is a most extraordinary animal; the stuffed specimens do not at all give a good idea of the [living] appearance of its head and beak; the latter becoming hard and contracted.

A little before this I had been lying on a sunny bank, and was reflecting on the strange character of the animals of this country as compared with the rest of the world. An unbeliever in every thing beyond his own reason might exclaim, 'Two distinct Creators must have been at work; their object, however, has been the same, and certainly the end in each case is complete.' While thus thinking, I observed the hollow conical pitfall of the lion-ant: first a fly fell down the treacherous slope and immediately disappeared; then came a large but unwary ant; its struggles to escape being very violent, those curious little jets of sand, described by Kirby as being flirted by the insect's tail, were promptly directed against the expected victim. But the ant enjoyed a better fate than the fly, and escaped the fatal jaws which lay concealed at the base of the conical hollow. There can be no doubt but that this predacious larva belongs to the same genus with the European kind, though to a different species. Now what would the sceptic say to this? Would any two workmen ever have hit upon so beautiful, so simple, and yet so artificial a contrivance. It cannot be thought so; one Hand has surely worked throughout the universe.

January 20. A long day's ride to Bathurst. Before joining the high road we followed a mere path through the forest; and the country, with the exception of a few squatters' huts, was very solitary. A 'squatter' is a freed, or 'ticket of leave' man, who builds a hut with bark on unoccupied ground, buys or steals a few animals, sells spirits without a licence, receives stolen goods, and so at last becomes rich and turns farmer: he is the horror of all his honest neighbours. A 'crawler' is an assigned convict who runs away, and lives how he can, by labour and petty theft. The 'bush ranger' is an open villain, who subsists by highway robbery and plunder; generally he is desperate, and will sooner be killed than taken alive. In the country it is necessary to understand these three names, for they are in common use.

    This day we experienced the sirocco-like wind of Australia, which comes from the parched deserts of the interior. Clouds of dust were travelling in every direction; and the wind felt like that which had passed over a fire. I afterwards heard that the thermometer out of doors stood at 119 degrees, and in a room in a closed house at 96 degrees [48

and 36 degrees celsius]. In the afternoon we came in view of
the downs of Bathurst. These undulating but nearly level plains
are very remarkable in this country, from being absolutely
destitute of a single tree. They support only a very thin brown
pasture. We rode some miles across this kind of country, and
then reached the township of Bathurst, which is seated in the
middle of what may be called either a very broad valley or
narrow plain.

Bathurst has a singular and not very inviting appearance. Groups of small houses and a few large ones are
scattered rather thickly over two or three miles of a bare country, which is divided into numerous fields by lines of rails. A
good many gentlemen live in the neighbourhood, and some
possess very comfortable houses. A hideous little red brick
church stands by itself on a hill; and barracks and government buildings occupy the centre of the township. I was told
not to form too bad an opinion of the country by judging
from that on the road-side, nor too good a one from Bathurst;
in this latter respect I did not feel myself in the least danger of
being prejudiced. It must be confessed that the season had
been one of great drought, and that the country did not wear
a favourable aspect; although I understand it was incompara-
bly worse two or three months before. The secret of the
rapidly growing prosperity of Bathurst is that the brown
pasture which appears to the stranger's eye so wretched is
excellent for sheep-grazing.

The town stands on the banks of the Macquarie: this
is one of the rivers whose waters flow into the vast and scarcely
known interior. The line of watershed, which divides the
inland streams from those of the coast, has an elevation of
about 3,000 feet (Bathurst is 2,200) and runs in a north and
south direction at the distance of about eighty or a hundred
miles from the sea-side. The Macquarie figures in the map as
a respectable river, and is the largest of those that drain this
part of the inland slope; yet to my surprise I found it a mere
chain of ponds, separated from each other by spaces almost
dry. Generally a small stream is running, and sometimes there
are high and impetuous floods. Scanty as the supply of the

water is throughout the district, it becomes still scantier further inland.

January 22. I commenced my return, and followed a new road, called Lockyer's Line [to Bowenfels via O'Connell and Tarana], in which the country is rather more hilly and picturesque. This was a long day's ride; and the house where I wished to sleep was some way off the road, and not easily found. I met on this, and indeed on all other occasions, a very general and ready civility among the lower orders; which, when one considers what they are, and what they have been, would scarcely have been expected. The farm where I passed the night was owned by two young men who had only lately come out, and were beginning a settler's life. The total want of almost every comfort was not very attractive; but future and certain prosperity was before their eyes, and that not far distant.

The next day we passed through large tracts of country in flames, volumes of smoke sweeping across the road. Before noon we joined our former track, and ascended Mount Victoria. I slept at the Weatherboard, and before dark took another walk to the amphitheatre. On the road to Sydney I spent a very pleasant evening with Captain King at Dunheved: and thus ended my little excursion in the colony of New South Wales.

IX

Louisa Meredith

Over-liberal libations

L ouisa Meredith, English-born author and illustrator, wrote two volumes of verse and a travel book before coming to Australia. Soon after her arrival, in 1839, she made this crossing of the mountains.

On quitting Parramatta we passed near Government House, which is beautifully situated in a fine domain, and frequently visited by the governor. Sir Maurice O'Connell, commander of the forces in Australia, now resides there. The road to Penrith passes occasionally through pleasant scenery, though chiefly monotonous enough, and the intense heat made me almost incapable of enjoying anything; added to which, the indescribable chirruping, creaking and whirring of myriads of grass-hoppers (dust-hoppers more properly), that seemed to fill all space around us, was almost intolerable, and what was very extraordinary, these unwelcome musicians were wholly invisible, nor could the most rigid observation detect them ...

Early the following morning we resumed our journey, in company with a friend with whom we had arranged to travel the remainder of the way. Ourselves, carriages, and horses were safely ferried over the Nepean in a large punt, or railed raft, and landed on the opposite bank, when we drove merrily along the Emu Plains, so named no doubt from the flocks of emu formerly found there; but as civilized, and therefore doubly destructive, man advances in a new country, he invariably exterminates or scares away the timid creatures that have for ages dwelt there undisturbed; and now these noble birds have become unknown, except in the almost untrodden districts of the interior. I saw two tamed ones in a part of the government domain at Sydney; they are most noble-looking birds, and seemed quite happy in the comparative freedom they enjoyed. Their eggs are of a rich dark green colour, with a rough surface, like the rind of a coarse orange, or shagreen, and are about the size of those of an ostrich, which bird the emu resembles in general appearance, though handsomer and less awkward.

We had a fine view of the long range of the Blue Mountains before us, and of the abrupt gorge through which the Nepean flows before reaching Penrith. This pass is described as being extremely grand on a nearer approach, as indeed it must be, from the perpendicular height of the mountains, and the large volume of water pouring through so narrow a channel.

After driving for about two miles over the level plains, we reached the foot of Lapstone Hill, the first ascent, up which an excellent road has been made, winding along the side of the mountain, with high overhanging rocks on the left hand and a deep wooded ravine on the right. The wild scenery and the zigzag road reminded me of some of the 'passes of the Alps', as drawn by Brockedon, save that our ravine had no foaming torrent roaring down it; and it was only by most intent observation that I could detect something like moisture trickling over the rocks, where an opening in the trees left the far-down stony bed visible.

It was October, and, as I have before remarked, the spring months are by far the greenest in this land of ever-browns; so that I saw the country under rather favourable circumstances, although the severe droughts of the two preceding years had destroyed the artificial crops, and even the native grasses, to a deplorable extent. Still, among these lofty mountains and in their shady recesses the trees and shrubs grew in unchecked luxuriance, and yielded me many a new and beautiful flower. As we slowly wound up the steep ascent, and the folding hills narrowed the view behind us, the scene was most picturesque and striking. Far on before us we could see the white-gleaming road still climbing higher and higher; looking back, the plains, reduced to a triangular section by the closing hills, were fast receding from the landscape; gigantic crags, piled high overhead, were mingled with an endless variety of tree, shrub and flower; and far below, from the depths of the ravine, the opposite side of the pass rose almost perpendicularly, till its upper trees seemed to cut against the bright, unclouded, blue sky. I was quite delighted, and thought that if all our progress over the dreaded Blue Mountains were as pleasant and interesting as the commencement, the journey would be much less wearisome than I anticipated.

I had often been told of the 'waratah' (*Telopea speciocissima*), and its grand appearance when growing; and as we drove along, instantly recognised from the description the first of these magnificent flowers we saw, and soon after came more into their especial region, which is about half-way up the height of the mountain, few being seen either above or below this range. From the temperature, I should think their cultivation at home would be easy, and it would well repay some pains to have such noble flowers added to the treasured wealth of English gardens. The stem is woody, and grows perfectly straight, from three to six feet in height, about the thickness of a walking cane, and bearing rich green leaves (something like those of the oak, but much larger) all the way up. At the top of this stem is the flower, entirely of the brightest and richest shade of crimson-scarlet. A circle of large spreading petals forms its base, from which rises the cone or pyramid of trumpet-like florets, three, four, or five inches high; the whole flower being much the size and shape of a fine artichoke. Sometimes the stems branch off like a candelabrum, but more generally the flowers grow singly, one on each stalk, and look like bright flambeaux amidst the dark recesses of these wild forests. Unfortunately I had no opportunity of making a drawing of one, having no materials at hand on our journey, and failed to procure a flower during our stay in Sydney. The few plates I have seen give but a very faint idea of this most stately and regal flower.

After driving for some miles nearly all up-hill, we stayed to breakfast at a small way-side publichouse, where the slovenly slipshod women, dirty floors, and a powerful odour of stale tobacco-smoke, gave me no very favourable expectations of cleanliness or comfort. On the smoke-stained walls hung some very highly coloured and showily framed prints, representing young gentlemen with red cheeks and very blue coats trying to look very hard at young ladies in pink gowns with very large sleeves; and severally inscribed, 'The Faithful Lovers', 'The Betrothed', 'The False One', &c.; ingenious distinctions of character, which it would have been extremely difficult to discover from the portraits alone.

In many places you find some particular dish more generally in vogue than others, but in New South Wales one universal reply follows the query of 'What can you give us to eat?' and this is, *'Am an' eggs, Sir,* mutton chops forming the usual accompaniment, if required. So ham and eggs we had, and mutton chops, too; but from their being fried all together in the same dark-complexioned fat, the taste of these viands was curiously similar, and both of impenetrable hardness. Unless great care is taken, meat spoils so soon in this climate that the custom among most persons is to cook it almost as soon as killed, which of course precludes the possibility of it being tender. Tea, with black sugar but no milk, and bread without butter, completed the repast, with the addition of 'damper', a composition respecting which there are divers opinions, some persons preferring it to bread, whilst I think it the worst way of spoiling flour. The etymology is perhaps 'Dampier,' this indigestible food (an excellent damper of a good appetite) being supposed by some persons to have been invented by the great circumnavigator, and the manufacture is this: a stiff dough is made of flour, water, and salt, and kneaded into a large flat cake, two or three inches thick, and from twelve to eighteen broad. The wood-ashes are then partially raked from the hot hearth, and the cake being laid on it, is heaped over the remaining hot ashes, and thus baked. When cut into, it exceeds in closeness and hard heaviness the worst bread or pudding I ever tasted, and the outside looks dirty, if it is not so, still, I have heard many persons, conversant with every comfort and luxury, praise the 'damper', so I can only consider my dislike a matter of taste. In 'the bush', where brewer's yeast cannot be procured, and people are too idle or ignorant to manufacture a substitute for it (which is easily done), this indurated dough is the only kind of bread used, and those who eat it constantly must have an ostrich's digestion to combat its injurious effects ...

'Mais revenons à nos moutons!'—We continued our journey through a wild and barren country, utterly destitute of herbage; the inhospitable Blue Mountains were before, behind, and on either side of us, rising in grand and dreary monotony of form and colour. Forests of tall gum trees covered them from base to peak, but instead of a beauty in the landscape, these were a deformity. All bore the marks of fire far up their branchless, blackened stems, and in many places the burning had been so recent, that for miles the very earth seemed charred, and not even a stunted shrub had sprung up again. The trees, huge masses of charcoal to all appearance, had no branches till very near the summit, and these bore only a few scattered tufts of rusty leaves, scarcely casting a visible shadow, and affording no shade. The steepest ravines had not the semblance of water in their dry dreary depths, and but for the fearful quagmires and deep holes in the road (which made the utmost care in driving requisite to avoid an upset over the precipice), one would not have thought that rain or dew ever visited this desert region.

The main portion of the road is *bad* beyond an English comprehension; sometimes it consists of natural step-like rocks protruding from the dust or sand one, two or three feet above each other, in huge slabs the width of the track, and over these 'jumpers', as they are pleasantly termed, we had to jolt and bump along as we best might. How our springs stood such unwonted exercise is an enigma still; but as a vehicle of the barouche species, crammed in every imaginable corner with live freight and luggage, had passed the inn whilst we were at breakfast, I am inclined to think that springs in colonial use must be made of sterner stuff than I had hitherto given them credit for.

The track we were now traversing usually winds terrace-wise along the side of a steep mountain, and is barely wide enough anywhere to allow of two vehicles passing each other. All the produce of the settlers in the upper country is conveyed to Sydney by this road, and farm supplies taken up from thence: therefore it is no uncommon thing to meet a train of six or eight heavily laden drays (for the continual depredations of bush-rangers render it advisable that several should travel in company), each drawn by eight, ten or twelve oxen; and to encounter such a caravan on the narrow mountain road is by no means a desirable incident. The patience and docility of the ox are justly proverbial, but unfortunately colonial drivers are less gifted with these virtues, and their violence, ill-temper, and brutal usage often seem to bewilder the poor weary creatures, who, having no harness but bows and yokes, twist round and entangle themselves, much to their own peril and that of any passing horses or carriages. We once narrowly escaped a serious accident from this cause, by driving down the bank, steep as it was, out of the way.

Two years of desolating drought had preceded our arrival in Sydney, and the melancholy proofs of its ravages among the brute creation met us here at every turn, in the remains of unfortunate oxen that had perished of want in their toilsome journeys over the mountains, where neither food nor water remained for them; and as the dray-journeys from the distant stations to Sydney occupy from three to six weeks, the lingering, protracted misery endured, even by the wretched animals who survived, is horrible to contemplate. In some places by the road-side white skeletons alone remained; farther on we saw other carcasses still covered with hide; then bones again; and so on, continually meeting these terrible proofs of the poor brutes' sufferings and death. It recalled to my mind descriptions I have read of the caravan-tracks in the sandy deserts of Africa, where the bleached bones of animals that have perished in the journey serve as guides to future travellers.

The climate changed materially as we gained the higher regions of the mountains, becoming quite cold, and I gladly wrapped up in cloaks and furs; our companion, who usually drove within hail of us, retired into a grotesque cloak-hood-and-coat sort of garment, made of the thick furry opossum skins of the colony, and looked like an exaggerated Esquimaux, as we caught a glimpse of his portly figure now and then through the thick flurries of sleety rain that swept round us, the sudden squalls being too furious for any umbrella to live in them. So, laughing merrily (when the wind did not take our breath away), we drove briskly on, our destination for the night being the 'Weatherboard' inn [at Wentworth Falls] (so named from its being built, like many houses in the colony, wholly of wood, the walls consisting of thin boards lapped one over another, nailed to upright slabs or posts, and lathed and plastered within). What was my dismay, as I was just ready to alight, cold, tired and hungry, at the door of this mountain refuge for the destitute, on our being informed that the house was full, and not a sleeping-place to be had! A native settler returning from Sydney to Bathurst with his wife and family were in possession of all the accommodation. These were the occupants of the loaded carriage I had seen, who, with more foresight than ourselves, had pushed on as rapidly as possible in advance, and seized upon the whole establishment. After a short debate it was determined to go on six miles farther, to a smaller hostel, known as 'Blind Paddy's' [just beyond Katoomba], though it was nearly dark and raining fast. However, on we went, 'through bush and through brier,' to say nothing of holes and rocks in the road; and in the process of time, long after dark, reached our little inn, very wet, and colder, and hungrier than ever. A couple of decent elderly women appeared to do the honours, and ushered us into a small but clean whitewashed room, gaily adorned with feathers, shells, and the droll little pictures usually found in such houses; a bright wood-fire was soon crackling and blazing merrily on the white hearth; the homely table was quickly spread with a coarse but snowy cloth, and supper most expeditiously prepared, consisting of the never-failing dish 'ham and eggs,' chops, damper, tea, and—crowning luxury of all— a dish of hot mealy potatoes, smiling most charmingly through their cracked and peeling skins. Wine in such houses as this is rarely drinkable, but excellent English ale (at 3s. 6d. per quart bottle) is generally found in them, so that our repast was by no means contemptible, and the air of plain homely cleanliness about the arrangements added to all an unwonted relish.

A tolerable night's rest in a room about the size of our ship-cabin, with a clean dimity bed and window curtains, and no worse nocturnal visitants than a moderate party of the universal 'light infantry', left me quite recruited and ready for setting forth again on our onward journey, after a breakfast very similar to our supper, or rather dinner, of the preceding evening.

Our route still lay through the same wild, monotonous scenery as the day before. The sight of vast mountain-ranges spread all around, folding in and behind each other as they filled all space, could not be otherwise than *grand* in the extreme, but it was most dreary, desolate grandeur. Trees without foliage, hills and valleys alike destitute of verdure, chasms and ravines yawning beside us, without a thread of water in their arid, stony depths, made up such a world of desolation that the contemplation of it became absolutely oppressive, and I gladly listened to glowing descriptions of the green and beautiful plains of Bathurst, which we were to reach the following day.

In one place we came to an almost precipitous descent in the road, called 'Soldier's Pinch' or 'Pitch', most probably from some accident which has happened there. It was a mass of loose stones, continually rolling from under the horses' feet, and so steep as to be very fatiguing even to walk down, which I preferred doing, not being quite reconciled to such roads for driving on. At the foot lay huge masses and heaps of wood, trees of all sizes having been hooked on to the drays at the summit of the Pitch, to prevent their rushing down suddenly, despite locked wheels, and overrunning the unfortunate oxen. If Major Mitchell, when Colonial Surveyor, had turned his attention and directed his men's labour to such places as this, and remedied their dangerous character, he would have rendered great and essential service to the colonists; but in the generality of instances his road has been made where a *good* bush-track formerly existed, and the really bad and dangerous portions remain in very many instances untouched—at least such was the case when I crossed the mountains. I could not avoid noticing likewise, that Major Mitchell's road, wherever originally marked by him, was almost invariably carried over the summits of hills, whilst level valleys lay within a few hundred feet; and as we proceeded, I looked out for the highest peaks ahead of us, knowing by experience that the surveyor's road would lead us over them. I was informed that a determination to adopt no other person's suggested line of road was the reason of this most inconvenient and fatiguing route being resolved on, and I have since heard that a new survey is to be made, and a more level and rational track marked out.

The only portion of the present road for which I can give Major Mitchell great credit is the Pass of Mount Victoria … A large gang of convicts were stationed here road-making, and several of them importuned us for money or tobacco, showing such truly villainous countenances that the idea of being waylaid by bush-rangers gained tenfold horrors, and the knowledge that many were out made me often look very earnestly at a misshapen gum-log or crooked tree, fancy transforming it to 'a highwayman, with pistols as long as my arm.' In one place, we met a couple of soldiers in search of some newly-escaped convicts; they were running about in a half-stooping position, peeping and thrusting their fixed bayonets into every thin bush and low tussock of grass where a man could not by any possibility be hidden, with most valorous resolves no doubt, but cutting rather a ludicrous figure. I am not aware if they succeeded in their chase, but have strong suspicions that they did not.

A comparatively level road succeeded to the grand mountain pass, and we journeyed on to our mid-day resting place, called the 'Rivulet,' the little stream at this place being by some remarkable accident rightly named. A new, glaringly smart-looking inn here promised tolerable accommodation; it was as fine as twenty different coloured kinds of paint could make it. Panellings and 'pickings-out' of rainbow hues were set off by pillars of imitative and varnished marble, the like of which no quarry ever knew; and these again touched up with bronze-paint and gilding, gleamed in the sun with almost dazzling lustre. A good verandah led by French windows to the two front rooms, into which I walked, without seeing any inhabitants or attendants. A few gaudily painted chairs, a small bad mirror in a large gilt frame thickly shrouded in yellow gauze, and a new cedar table covered with tobacco-ashes and liquor-stains, composed the furniture of either apartment. After a long and ineffectual sonata on the hand-bell (no other description being seen, save in a very few of the very best colonial houses), just as I began to despair of its power, a young girl shuffled along the hall from some of the back settlements, and holding fast by the door-handle, for she was almost too much intoxicated to stand, took my orders for luncheon, and after many vain attempts at length succeeded in wiping the table with a ragged, very dirty apron. Her dull light-coloured hair hung in matted tangles about her neck and ears; her dress was disordered, torn and dirty; and her face bloated and stupid from the effects of drink; never did drunkenness wear a more revolting aspect, and I felt relieved when the wretched creature left the room. My companions had a similar tale to tell of the male portion of the establishment; every soul was drunk, and it was some time before they could arouse anyone to attend to the horses. The same unfortunate girl I had before seen laid our cloth, and brought what we wanted, or rather what we could get, for I imagine the copious libations indulged in by the whole household had made them regardless of eating, and the larder was accordingly very ill supplied. Bread and a few eggs (positively without ham!), which our ministering Bacchante rolled on the floor as she staggered in with them, formed our repast, but she took pains to impress upon us the pleasing assurance that 'There was plenty o' ale an' sperrits.'

We strolled down to the banks of the little rivulet, where I found many beautiful flowering shrubs, and the verdure of the adjacent little flats showed how excellent a garden might be made there, but I fear never will; idleness and drinking are such besetting sins, and money to provide them both so easily earned by 'keeping a public' in this colony, that nothing demanding bodily exertion is attempted. Meat can run about and feed itself on the wild hills, and flour they can buy; fruit and vegetables they 'don't heed', as they would demand some little labour to produce.

As we returned towards the house, I looked at it again, as it stood in raw, shiny, comfortless newness, like a great toy freshly unpacked. Behind it lay a crowd of dirty, old, ruinous hovels, that formerly served in its stead, and still were used as outhouses, stables, &c., all broken, and half un-thatched. All the fences within sight exhibited the same dilapidated aspect, whilst ash-heaps and other less sightly things lay all around. How different would be the state of almost everything in this colony, were that greatest curse man ever created out of God's good gifts, intoxicating liquor, less easily obtained by those who *ought* to be the industrious and prosperous, but, alas! too generally *are* the idle and worthless part of the community. Time, money, character, decency, feeling, principle, ambition, and honesty—all are sacrificed to the demoralizing passion for rum, when once it gains the ascendancy; and to know how often that is, we need only observe and listen to the sad evidence so continually passing around us. I perhaps praise the tidy appearance and good cookery of a friend's servant: 'Ah! yes, she is an excellent cook, but we can so seldom keep her *sober*.' The coachman of another seems quite a model for his class, till you hear he is so confirmed a drunkard that his mistress dares not trust him to drive her home alone from a party. Another family have an honest old 'major-domo', faithful and good in every other point; may be trusted with 'untold gold,' but not with a bottle of rum. It is a universal failing, and a really sober servant or mechanic may consequently be held as a pearl of great price. Age and sex make no difference; your dainty lady's maid or pretty young nurse-girl is just as likely to be over-liberal in her libations to Bacchus as your groom or shoeblack; and no threats, no bribes, no punishments avail to keep the besotted creatures from the dram-bottle, if it be by any means or in any shape accessible. I have known a female servant drink camphorated spirits of wine, and suspect the same individual of consuming a pint of hartshorn which mysteriously disappeared about the same time from my room; its evident strength being no doubt too tempting. Eau de Cologne and lavender-water, I know, they drink whenever they are left about, or anything else believed to contain spirit.

The universality of this vice is most dreadful to contemplate, and far worse to witness and endure. Almost the only exceptions among the lower classes are the families of English emigrants, who, accustomed to poor living and hard work at home, continue sober and industrious, thankful for the many hitherto unknown comforts and luxuries they can enjoy, and carefully and fearfully abstaining from all excesses. Of this class I have known excellent examples, both young and old, male and female, and can only hope that in time their better and wiser course may be appreciated and emulated by other portions of this now numerous population.

Our road now lay over hilly ground again, sometimes skirted by live trees and a slight semblance of herbage, and often approaching in wild and sterile grandeur the scenery we had before traversed. A singular range of perpendicular cliffs form a striking feature in the landscape at a place called 'Hassan's Walls'. These walls or cliffs rise, I should think, to a height of about three hundred feet perpendicularly above the road, and their summits, broken and fissured in various fantastic forms, exactly resemble a ruined castle crowning the brow of the sheer precipice, with here and there a stunted tree or graceful shrub growing from crevices in the dark rock. Had I been travelling in an old country, I should at once have decided that these were truly the ruins of some mighty mountain-fortress of former days; loop-holes, arches, battlements and buttresses were, as it seemed, so clearly remaining, and extending far along the airy heights of these genii-haunted crags, for such I half fancied them, especially when a turn in the road gave to view a colossal head standing well out against the clear, bright, blue sky, and bearing a strong resemblance to the venerable and veteran Duke of Wellington. We paused to contemplate the rude, though striking likeness; and then, as we slowly drove on, the features changed, and a judge with a flowing wig stood frowning down on us; another turn, and another change came over the mountain statue, and then it again resolved itself into a mere turret of the hoary ruin ...

The next point of our route having any claim to the picturesque was the rocky ravine at Cox's River; the sight of clear running water is always pleasant, but nowhere more delightful than in so dry and thirsty a clime as this. The ruins of numerous huts, formerly occupied by a convict-gang at this spot, gave it rather a desolate look; but the clear little brook (for such in England should we call this river) gurgling merrily over its pebbly bed, had a sweet music in its voice that made me forget all disagreeables. We tasted and then crossed it, and immediately began the steep ascent of Mount Lambie, which rises abruptly from the river's bank. This mount had been the highest point in our landscape all day, and accordingly, despising all humbler and easier tracks, over its very summit passes Major Mitchell's vaunted road. Seven long miles of climbing were before us, up as bare, sterile a mountain as ever gloomed on a wayfarer's path. The rock is a splintery slate, not unlike many in old south and north Wales, and its dark grey and purple hue, stained in places with a rusty tinge, gave a dismal monotony to the scene, which scarcely a shrub or herb appeared to relieve.

An inn has very wisely been built half-way up this

inhospitable mountain, and there, at the auspicious sign of
the Queen Victoria, we purposed remaining the night, which
was fast approaching, for the rapid departure of twilight leaves
little time after sunset available for travelling. After a weary
pull of four miles, the gracious countenance of our fair Queen
(somewhat libelled by the artist, it is true) beamed on our
most loyal and rejoiced eyes from amidst a chaos of crown,
sceptre, red drapery and ermine; and our tired horses, after a
last resolute effort, stopped at the inn door. At the same moment we heard a handbell sharply and loudly rung within,
and after a minute's delay the landlord appeared at our sum-
mons, with the pleasing intelligence that he was very sorry
indeed, but he could not accommodate us. As it was
impossible to proceed farther in this case, there being no other
habitation within a long stage, and our horses knocked up,
Mr. Meredith and Mr. Campbell declared their determination to stay at all events; and again questioned the landlord,
who then admitted his own willingness to receive us (and
who of his class ever voluntarily rejected good customers?),
which he could easily do at some trifling inconvenience, but
Mrs. — (whose party had the preceding evening excluded us
from the 'Weatherboard') was there, and the instant we stopped
had *ordered* that no one else should be admitted, as they had
taken *all the house!* This most overbearing monopoly, however, did not prevent our being comfortably installed in a
snug little parlour, and a tolerable bed-room, which some of
the landlord's family vacated for us, whilst a sofa in the sit-
ting-room was made up into a bed for our companion. I am
well aware that had we been known at the time, the conduct
of this 'lady' would have been very different; but at such an
hour, and in such a place, no woman possessed of common
humanity would have desired to turn a beggar from the door.
The pride of wealth, unmixed with aught of better or nobler
feeling, is too often the sole and engrossing principle and
characteristic of persons raised by some fortunate chance to
that kind of rank which in these Colonies, where the worship of Mammon reigns triumphantly, is at once accorded to
the *rich*: 'What *has* he?' not 'What *is* he?' being the test; and

this petty superiority is often the foundation of absurd and selfish importance, of which the above trifling incident is an apt illustration.

I am happy to say we found the members of this royal establishment sober, industrious, and civil; a most welcome contrast to the inn at the Rivulet, and, despite our unpropitious reception, were tolerably comfortable.

Editor's note: Surveyor George Evans, who had trouble with his spelling, actually named the stream beyond Mount York the River Lett, the name it bears today.

X

Sophia Stanger

Five dear babes

The experience of crossing the Blue Mountains was changed for ever by the building of the railway in the 1860s. In 1882 a Bathurst printer published the following letter, from Sophia Stanger, who in 1841 had crossed the mountains with her husband and five children, to her mother in England. According to the introduction to the letter, 'To those who may have to face similar difficulties in pushing into the still farther interior, it may show what patience, perseverance, and industry, as here recorded, trusting also to the care and guidance of an all wise Providence, will accompany those who determine to make a home for themselves and their families in this beautiful (almost boundless) and free country.'

⟶∙◦∙⟶ ⟶∙◦∙⟶

Bathurst, N.S.W.
July 15th, 1841

My own Beloved Mother:
The most speedy mode of travelling over the mountains is by

the mail cart, which leaves Sydney for Bathurst on certain days, but this is too expensive to be generally adopted, as the lowest fare is 90/- each person; all therefore, who cannot afford this, and have no conveyance of their own, are under the necessity of travelling by some of the drays, numbers of which are constantly on the road to and from Sydney.

After many anxieties respecting this journey, it was settled that our best plan would be to dispose of many unnecessary articles we had in possession, and purchase in their stead the most useful and saleable in the part we were bound for. These were packed with all our other goods on bullock drays, and with a person who had purchased land at King's Plains and wished to see it, we agreed that he should take us in his own dray with two horses, and our bedding and provisions for the journey. These drays are precisely the same as those used by the small brewers in England. We had hoped, by this arrangement, to have had sufficient room, to have travelled the distance in a week, and to have escaped the very undesirable company of the bullock drivers, who are almost sure to be convicts of the very lowest grade.

After this agreement was made, our driver, wishing to make the journey as advantageous to himself as possible, loaded the dray with various commodities of a bulky and weighty character, paying no regard to our comfort or that of the horses.

And now, dear mother, fancy me with my five dear babes seated on the top of this miserable load! Eliza walking on a little out of the town, and my husband by our side, on one of the coldest mornings in June (which you must remember is your November, and quite as cold in many parts); but, although we had resolved on *starting*, the poor horses had evidently determined otherwise, both positively refusing to act as leader. After much whipping, scolding, and rearing up, the horse in the shafts fell down, with the load pressing heavily on some part of it, making it very restive, and with no little difficulty we again dismounted. As is usual in such cases, we soon had plenty of help, and I plenty of advisers:

'Sure you wouldn't be thinking to cross the mountains with all those children!' cried one; and, 'Sure you'll lose all your babes, God bless them!' cried another; and, 'The mountains all covered with snow, you will certainly perish,' said a third; while others were utterly astonished the young girl should have so many children, and especially *three* at a birth! But we believed it our duty to proceed, and to Him who had borne us in safety over the seas we looked for protection on the mountains.

Every hour seemed now to increase our perplexities, for the horses would not stir an inch, and the load was by far too heavy. Our goods were gone on several days in advance of us, and there we stood with just money enough to defray our expenses and none to spare for delays or fresh agreements, the driver coolly telling us that he was very sorry, but his horses would not take the load, and he would not go without it.

It was in the midst of these troubles that I thought my poor husband's courage would have failed him, and never shall I forget his look when with eyes filled with tears (not allowed to escape), he exclaimed, 'Dear, what *am* I to do!' About mid-day, however, we bade farewell to Sydney, the driver having procured another dray and horses, dividing the goods between them. Owing to the roads being heavy after a fortnight's rain, we made but eight miles that day, and as there was no food or water for our horses, we drove into an inn yard. Now you must not expect it was one of those comfortable places so common in dear Old England, where, after the fatigues of this troublous day, we might have been accommodated at a reasonable rate, but finding that £4 at the lowest would have been the demand, our drays were drawn carefully under a shed, and for the first time in our lives with sorrowful hearts we began to prepare our beds on the top, contrary to the usual mode which is *under* the drays. I dare say you can believe we slept but little—poor Mary and Sarah both fell from the top, the latter's fall somewhat modified by coming in contact with the dog. There would have been no danger of their falling out at all, but Eliza, not finding as much room as she had been used to, had slipped into the manger, where she slept peacefully for an hour or two, till the man, who had located himself somewhere in the neighbourhood, arose to feed his cattle, and mistaking her cap for the corn sack, handled it rather too unceremoniously. At daybreak we again started, but surely no Sabbath ever dawned and found us less prepared to welcome it. As the roads were better, we reached Parramatta by noon, and by night found ourselves fully 18 miles from Sydney, and stopped at a beer shop, which affording no hospitable shed, we slept that night in the open air.

The next day we passed through Penrith, a pretty little village, at the end of which we were with the drays ferried across the Nepean (in a punt), a river about three hundred feet wide, and from which we first saw the Blue Mountains in all their magnificence. Here, filling our bottles with water, we proceeded over Emu Plains, and rested our horses at the foot of Lapstone Hill. Here we lighted our first fire, and seated around it in true gypsy style, partook of our first comfortable meal. Being anxious to reach the top before dark, we attempted once more to proceed, but here the poor horses again raised objections, and very soon the accompanying dray was backed fast in a tree, about nine feet below the level of the road, and here we must have stayed had not a number of men forming the iron-gang (who were returning from their work of improving these roads) kindly assisted us, for a small sum of money to buy themselves tobacco. They very readily strung into a harness of ropes, some drawing before, and others pushing at the wheels. These men are stationed at various places, with two or three soldiers over them, working constantly in heavy irons, and their labour generally appointed as a punishment.

Our road hitherto had borne the appearance of a shrubbery or pleasure ground, lying through beautiful evergreens, thickly interspersed with flowers of different hues, and many of them quite equal to those dear Aunt brings from Wandsworth. The pretty heath, called acacia, and sold in London in pots, grows here in abundance, and, I think, must be the same; but as we were strangers in this really lovely land, we could only guess at the names. Here we seldom met a creature, but now and then a column of smoke, rising from a hut of the roughest construction, convinced us we were not in a fairy land.

But no language of mine can describe to you the beauty of Lapstone Hill, with its overhanging rocks on our left hand, and its awful gullies on our right. Once in particular, near its summit, we looked at each other in amazement, for the sun, which shone brightly, had penetrated its deepest recesses, and lit up its waterfalls and foliage in matchless beauty; but while we passed slowly along Sol sunk behind the mountains to make your day, leaving us to shudder at what we had before admired.

In a short time we reached the huts, and were persuaded by the men to encamp for the night at this station. The soldiers were very kind, and gave the children a good tea in their quarters, while we lighted a large fire and prepared their beds in a tent which my dear husband had made for the journey, and pitched for the night. Here, not quite unmindful of the company surrounding us, it was decided that the pistols should be loaded, and Joseph and the man act alternately as sentinels through the night. With the exception of the horses breaking loose and pushing violently against our tent (which, though based on a rock, stood none the more firmly), and a little alarm by a smell of burning, which proved to be the drivers' night-camp, we arose somewhat refreshed, and once more pursued our route.

Now, again, the roads were heavy, and the drivers, notwithstanding every effort, were constantly mortified by the horses standing still, and then again lying quite down. Through this day poor Eliza walked on with dear baby, and I brought up the rear, and blocked the wheels at every stoppage, sometimes left half-a-mile behind, and then having to run as fast as possible to perform this new but somewhat irksome duty. Having made this day about eight miles, we encamped near a hut at Springwood, and, with mutual consent, the next morning, parted with our guide, who, placing the horses abreast, proceeded with his load, leaving us to wait some other conveyance.

Towards evening that day we were joined by five bullock teams, and as one had behind his dray a new and empty one, we agreed with him to take us to Bathurst. Among these vehicles was the one loaded with our goods, which we had passed on the road; but as they formed altogether a jolly company, and had been a week coming from Sydney, they thought well to 'spell' (as they termed it) another day; but while they were carousing, our stock of provisions were diminishing; and it was with cheerful hearts that, about eleven the next morning, we found ourselves on the road, comfortably seated in our new conveyance, and forming, as the procession moved slowly along, a formidable array—for, to every dray, there were about three men to swear at, beat, and take care of the bullocks, each team consisting of *nine*, and almost as many dogs. Now we had no more anxiety, for our cattle were sure though slow, and if any difficulty occurred, it was only to hook on some ten or eight others, and soon all was set right.

Nothing occurred worth relating until we encamped the second night, when, having all our fires lighted, the wind blowing very cold and high, took some of our sparks across the road, which soon communicated with the bush. We were amused by seeing it spread and blaze to a considerable extent. It is not unfrequently that in dry seasons the bush takes fire, spreading destruction for miles, burning down everything before it. I should say that on these mountains we felt the cold quite as severely as at any time I can remember in England, and we daily expected snow, as it lays sometimes for weeks on these ridges; but dear Joseph most cleverly contrived to shelter us by placing our ship's berths at the sides, and covering the top with the canvas of our tents.

It was late one evening when we began to descend Mount Victoria. At its top there is a very sudden and awkward hill, called Soldier's Pinch, which owes its name to the folly of a soldier, who, being called on to block the wheel, unwittingly placed his foot instead of a stone, which was, of course, crushed to atoms. At the bottom of Soldier's Pinch is another cluster of huts belonging to the Iron-gang Station. Here the poor creatures all came out with the hope of buying tobacco, and to enquire if we were the people with the many children who had been set down on the mountains.

Our road now, for about two miles, was a gradual descent, the road good, and the scenery beautiful by the setting sun. And now we had reached the long-looked-for hill, which, report says, is like going down the side of a house, it being three miles long, and as steep as you can imagine. At the sight of it the most stout-hearted bullock driver owns that he shudders. In one part was a stone bridge about 150 yards long, and about three or four hundred feet above the level of the dell, which divides this mountain from another. In crossing this bridge, one now and then ventured to look over the slight parapet, and were pointed out the place where a wood-dray with three horses went over, and also the spot on which two men had fought, and the one thrown headlong by the fiend-like fury of his antagonist. Above the clouds Mount Victoria reared its craggy height, and looked defiance to all around; whilst beneath us, on both sides, appeared forests, and nearly fronting us Mount Haye, from which, by means of a telegraph, communications have been made with Sydney. I should have mentioned that at the top of this mountain, while the drivers locked their wheels, and yoked half their bullocks behind their loads, we took out the dear children (Eliza and I carrying one each, and their father, two, while dear Willie ran by their side). It was very near the bottom, with aching arms and weary feet we unanimously confessed it was far more pleasant to sit and read about mountains than to travel over them. It was almost dark when we camped, and had much difficulty in lighting our fires, as the wind was very high, and no water to be found within a mile.

At noon next day our bullocks were once more yoked, and we slowly climbed another mountain. The men, considering the worst of the journey was over, now began to drink rather freely; they had certainly treated us throughout with the greatest kindness and respect, but their general language is of a more awful and profane character than common English swearing. This part of our journey was beautiful in the extreme, and romantic beyond description. We greatly admired a particular kind of parrot; numbers of them were flying from tree to tree; they were very different from the common parrot, the colours being a bright mixture of red, green and blue. Our resting place this night was near to a public house by the side of a mountain, which was almost perpendicular. Through the kindness of our companions, we had here a nice supper of potatoes to eat with our last piece of meat, and in the morning some milk for the children, which, you must remember, is now a great treat.

In the middle of the next day the rain, which had threatened us long, now fell heavily, and soon dropped fast through our tent, which had formed a covering. In this miserable plight we again turned aside for the night. My husband here covered the tent with blankets, which are the best preventative against wet, and (pray, remember, should you be tempted while reading this to follow us here) we contrived to make our beds without getting out, dear Joseph waiting on us, drenched with rain and shivering with cold, for here it was quite impossible to light fires. This place is called Solitary Creek, and very solitary it is in wet weather! Through this night we had many fears, for the wind at times threatened nothing less than to upset us altogether.

In the morning we started again with a rather more favourable sky, but the roads in a most horrible state from the wet; sometimes our wheels sank to their axles—and then, oh, the beating! the shouting! and the swearing!! Here again through mud and mire we walked, and often, as the bullocks fell down or stuck fast, we carried the dear children. As there are no such roads in good old England, you can form no idea how really bad they are. Notwithstanding all that has been done to mend them, they remain, like Bunyan's 'Slough of Despond,' very little the better. This day, after many attempts, we succeeded in obtaining a loaf of bread, 4lbs. weight, for which we paid 2s. 6d.

The next day we came to Mount Lambie, and then our stock of provisions was fairly exhausted; for several days

we had watched them anxiously, and eaten them sparingly—
but now they were really gone, and had it not been that our
companions were kind, we must have fasted to Bathurst; but
Paddy, a steady convict for life, declared 'the women and children should not want while he had a morsel,' and brought us
a famous supply of potatoes. It seemed rather strange at first
sitting down to this truly Irish meal, but I assure you we all
ate heartily, and felt more thankful—I may safely add, than
we have often done when rising from an English breakfast of
bread, butter, and tea, with milk, to say nothing of the many
luxuries we often added, and which we now discovered as
needless.

After a similar breakfast next day, there was throughout the camp great washing, and shaving, and borrowing of
looking-glasses, as we were then but fourteen miles from
Bathurst, and hoped to reach it before sundown: all were
cheerful and busy, except my dear husband and I, for you
must not forget that sad inroads had been made upon our last
pound-note. As I have before said, our money had been
converted into goods (except what we had deemed necessary
to defray the expenses of our journey); these, as you may
suppose, were of a heavy kind, and for every hundredweight
we paid 12s. This is thought a very low price, for in dry
seasons it is as high as 25s.

Having met with such delay, and now with the un-
certainties of the way in which we could get from Bathurst
to King's Plains, and not knowing how long we might wait
there for a conveyance—camping is not allowed near the settlement—and public-house charges are exorbitant—and
friendless and unknown as we felt ourselves—we forgot that
our Heavenly Father who had never left or forsaken us in so
many troubles, was able to provide for us here; and before we
had decided which should be sold—my dear husband's watch
or mine, or the pistols—we reached Bathurst Plains, and read
the first milestone—eight miles from Bathurst. As my dear
husband has given a description of this settlement, I shall
hasten to say that, on entering it, our driver told us they
occupied a small cottage close by, and if we would like to

turn into it, they would sleep under the dray in the yard. This, of course, we joyfully accepted. After giving our dear children a comfortable tea, and thinking and saying how much better it would be in a smoky cottage, with broken windows and dirty floor, and cracks in the doors you might see through, than to be camping out, we set off to make a call on a Mr. Hughes.

The foreman of the Sydney Foundry, where my dear husband had been employed, had a daughter living with this person, and having a message from her mother, my dear husband thought he would do well to see Mr. Hughes, who was able to give his advice, his opinion being generally worth having. On our way we met the person who at first brought us from Sydney, and had just returned, and having heard that a quantity of drays were coming in, was then seeking us out to advise us by no means to proceed further, as it was not at all a suitable place for Mr. Stanger. He had seen Mr. Cooper, the younger, who, after hearing his description of him and his abilities, said he thought it would be quite inadvisable. Here again, as you might imagine, we were in a great dilemma, and earnestly trusting that Mr. Hughes might be enabled to guide us right, we reached his door, and were still more dismayed to find that he was out for some days. Mrs. Hughes, however, is a very pious, sensible and business-like woman, and, after hearing all said, she was quite certain it would be far better to stay in Bathurst, as there was just such a person needed, and advised my husband to go the next morning and judge of the place for himself, and by no means to take his family on until he had seen the man, who, as I before said, had brought goods, hoping to find a sale for them here. He had taken a room for a week, and as his sale was to take place next day, kindly offered us the use of it, as he must pay the week's rent for it. As the week did not end for four days, there was a place at once for us to go into, while my husband made his decisions free of any expense. To save time, he hired a horse, for which he paid 10/-, and the next morning started for the bush, leaving me to move from Paddy's cottage to the empty store; so once more packing our beds in the dray, and tying dear Willie on the top, Eliza and I took two children each and walked behind that nothing might be lost.

As that part of Bathurst to which we were bound was over the river, we had a favourable opportunity of viewing the place, which is beautifully romantic. After fording the river, we soon reached our destination, and here stood our goods, which, from all my husband had heard, he had thought best to detain. After helping the man to roll in some of the heavy casks—there being no fireplace—we begged hot water from our neighbours, and, giving the dear children a warm bath, all went to bed, and truly, dear mother, since I left my native land, I had never felt more depressed or forlorn, and my only consolation was as it had often been before, that *you* knew not what hardships your children were enduring. Here, dear Eliza did her utmost to comfort me, and trusting that soon our way would be made clear, at length fell asleep. Our repose was, however, soon broken by loud cries of 'murder,' and the eloquent voice of a coarse Irishwoman defying a man to open her box. As we were only separated by a glass door, you may suppose we were not a little alarmed for our best earthly protector was far away, and the only one left was a rough dog, which I had borrowed for the night and lay growling by my side. We soon found it was a sad quarrel between a man and his (should be) wife, who, after remonstrating with her for disturbing the free emigrants, gave her in charge, and left us thankful for the riddance.

The neighbours were kind in allowing us the use of their fires, but what we endured with cold you can scarcely imagine. The climate in this part is very much like that of England, and this is the depth of winter. About noon, my dear husband returned, and was never more welcomed. Three days after this, we were moved by our kind friend Mr. Hughes to the cottage and business my husband has mentioned, which, although humble, is peaceful and homelike compared to anything since we left. This we have made our Bethel, and with Jacob have vowed that now, 'if the Lord will bless us and find us food to eat and raiment to put on, and return us again to our Father's house, then he shall be our God, and the tenth of all we possess shall be His.'

You will not think we eat the bread of idleness when I tell you we have begun bonnet and dress making, and are called very clever. We are able to get just double the prices as at home, and as we are economical, and my husband's salary is good, he has, every week, a very pleasant little errand to the Bank; and so, dear mother, I hope we are very thankful, and trust we are just where we should be, as I do sometimes think that the prospect before us is rather cheering. We know 'the gold and the silver is the Lord's'. 'He also maketh rich, and addeth no sorrow thereto.' If spared, I will soon write another long letter about my dear darlings, whom we now look upon as wealth—for such they really are in this land— and I only regret that for a long time it will bear but poor interest. We only wish we could transplant many whom we are sure would do well. I often wish that dear Aunt Giffen and family had been advised by me and come with us. Shoes are very expensive, and they never think of mending.

Christopher, too, might do well, indeed, any one who cannot get on at home. Want is a thing never heard of here, and I assure you, an English family is made much of. I have never yet heard of any one who has not passed through many hardships on their first settling here, and we often feel thankful that we have been brought safely through this much of the portion assigned us. I long, dear mother, to see your handwriting—I wish you would write every month. I cannot, at times, suppress a tear, for although my dear husband has had many letters, I have received but one from B. and M. Tell Ellen she might, I am sure, write, for although the receipt of a letter generally unsettles us for days, still they are the greatest treat we have. We feel very much the loss of society, for such as we have been blessed with is very scarce. We are not so favoured as at Sydney with our minister, nor do we hear him with the pleasure or profit as we did Mr. Saunders, but we have found great friends in Wesleyans, and have every reason to love and speak well of them; besides, I hope, in this land, we have learnt to love all who love our common Lord,

Wheeny Creek, Wollemi National Park

Ferns and flowers

Coachwood

Leptospermum sp.

Banksia serrata leaves

Angophora bakerii

and can readily worship with any, whatever may be the form, for sectarianism has not yet ventured to cross the ocean, and foundered be the bark in which she sets sail! I shall think much of our dear Barbara in September; pray tell me of all when you write, and what the dear babe or babes are named? I am often anxious to hear about dear old George and Miss — , and hope that you will begin with Barbara, and end with James, giving every particular.

And now, dear mother, farewell. Remember at the throne of grace your exiled children; cherish the hope of one day seeing us return, and believe me

Your ever affectionate

Sophia.

XI

Dave Noble and the Wollemi Pine

Serious canyoners are among the last explorers of the earth. They seek out gorges and go down them by walking, swimming, floating on li-los, crawling, diving, jumping and abseiling. They like to be the first. In the Wollemi National Park, a wilderness of almost half a million hectares less than two hours' drive from Sydney, the canyoners pore over the blue lines on the map, and then seek them out. Aerial photography means that almost every creek in the area is on the map, but further knowledge of the creek, and the country around it, can only be achieved on foot.

Sometimes the canyoners, after a hard walk from the nearest road to the blue line they have selected, find only a trickle of water through a small, flat valley. Boring. But if they strike lucky, they find a deep, narrow gorge, maybe only a metre across at the top and forty metres deep. Into this slot in the earth, formed by the action of water cutting through soft sandstone for millions of years, they descend, to re-emerge hours, perhaps a day, later, downstream.

Down below it is cool—sometimes cold—and dim,

with lots of moss and ferns, still pools, yabbies and slimy logs. This is strenuous exploration but not on a large scale and not particularly heroic. It attracts those with an interest in natural science rather than thrill-seekers.

Canyoners find things, usually small things. Like bolts, screwed into the rocks so slings and ropes can be attached for descents. The vandals who leave the bolts there like to say they do it to help those who come after them, but the real reason is laziness. Bolts are hard to remove. They also create safety problems—later canyoners are tempted to use the bolts, but have no way of knowing how secure they are, how fatigued or worn the metal is. And even if every bolt in the wilderness were secure, each bolt is an announcement that the wilderness is not as wild as most canyoners would like it to be.

Bolts are proliferating. In 1996 sixteen were found on one trip in the Claustral Canyon, and nineteen in Mount Hay. Sometimes they are placed by the commercial operators who run eco-tours down the more accessible canyons. It makes their jobs easier even as it spoils the experience for others. Nowadays serious canyoners spend a bit of time to remove every bolt they find. There is a bolt war going on in the Blue Mountains.

It's not just bolts. Ropes to assist with descents are increasingly being left in position in the canyons used by the commercial operators. Again, safety issues arise: ropes grow old, wear out, snap. Serious canyoners remove all the ropes they find, and carry them back to civilization, along with the cigarette butts, punctured li-los and McDonald's wrappers found along the way. It's a sad fact that the more accessible canyons of the Blue Mountains are being destroyed, and not just by conscious vandalism—the hand-holds chipped out of the rocks, the sandstone blackened by campfires, the Exit signs painted on the stone walls. Church, Scout and bushwalking groups regularly take large groups of people with little knowledge of the bush into canyons to savour their beauty. These groups trample the moss and crush the yabbies, their faeces pollute the water. It's not always anybody's fault.

Serious canyoners stay away from the popular canyons now, aware of just how much they've deteriorated in the past decade. And yet, serious canyoners are aware of the damage they too can do: weed seeds carried in on socks, sand compacted by the first heavy tread of a hiking boot. So the wilderness—and Wollemi National Park is the largest wilderness area in New South Wales—grows less wild every day. But it's still wild enough for things to be found out there. Exciting things.

Dave Noble is one of the most knowledgeable canyoners in Australia. On leaving school in the 1980s he took to canyoning at first just as "a different way to go hiking" but soon became addicted to its particular combination of physical activity, exploration and difficulty. In the past decade or so he has been down three hundred canyons, from the narrow slots of Wollemi to the deep ravines of Kanangra-Boyd. This has given him an intimate knowledge of the unique granite and sandstone landscapes of the area with their labyrinths of valleys and cliffs, their bare rock faces and sclerophyll and rain forests. Combined with his university studies in park management and his work as a project officer for the N.S.W. National Parks and Wildlife Service (N.P.W.S.), this has given him an extensive awareness of the flora of the Blue Mountains.

One Saturday in August 1994 Noble and two friends set off towards a creek selected from the map. The Wollemi wilderness, where he was headed, was actually better known to white Australians a hundred years ago than it is today. Back then there were the small farmers on the edges of the wild whose farms often failed and were reclaimed by the bush, the prospectors and occasional miners, and the timber-cutters, who moved through most of the forests of eastern Australia in the nineteenth and early twentieth centuries. 'Wilderness', in New South Wales at least, is partly a twentieth century creation. Noble and his friends carried daypacks and a full accompaniment of climbing and other gear. After parking their car they headed through the bush towards the top of the canyon, into which they abseiled. They walked downstream for several hours until the canyon opened out into a fairly narrow valley some six hundred metres deep, with walls going up in stages, those at the bottom being about fifty metres high. The area was almost pristine wilderness, inhabited by wallabies, scrub turkeys and lyrebirds. The ridges and valley walls had a light cover of dry sclerophyll forest dominated by gum trees, but the floor and low sides of the canyon, as often happens in the area, were home to warm temperate rain forest, dominated by Coachwood and Sassafras. It was here, walking near the bottom of the valley, that Noble was struck by some strange 'litter' on the ground.

This was not McDonald's wrappers but dead branches. Looking up, Noble saw that they had fallen from a number of tall pine trees which grew up through the rain forest canopy. Standing on wet, rocky ledges on the side of the valley, the trees were about 35 metres high with trunks a metre in diameter at their base. Their foliage varied from lime to apple green. Moving closer, he saw that the trunks were covered with an unusual bark, which looked like Coco Pops. He could not identify the tree, but made the reasonable assumption that it was a species introduced from outside the area, perhaps by a bird flying over the valley. He took a specimen, placed it in his pack, and moved on down the valley. It was a thin branch, about twenty centimetres long, with two rows of narrow leaves coming off it.

So unmoved was Noble by his find that he half forgot about it on his return home, only taking it from his pack and looking it up a few days later. Neither he nor his father, a keen conservationist, could identify the small branch, so he took it to work and left it on the desk of Wyn Jones, the naturalist at the Blackheath N.P.W.S. office near Govett's Leap. Jones thought it looked ordinary enough, and put it to the side of his desk, telling Noble he'd have a close look later.

In the early 1980s Jones had been the senior naturalist for the entire Central Region of the N.P.W.S., which stretches from the coast as far west as Parkes. Then he grew sick and decided he'd had enough of the city, and moved to his present part-time job in the mountains. He wanted to regain his love of the bush and to concentrate on his work with rare species. "It was almost a godsend when I got sick," Jones has said. In 1992 he went to America to perform an ancient Indian isolation ritual. "It was basically a way of becoming one with the land." He also organised a heritage walk through the Blue Mountains, from Sandy Hollow at the top of Wollemi National Park to Mittagong to the south of the Nattai National Park, to arouse people's interest in the preservation of the several dozen rare species of plants then known to exist in the Blue Mountains. For two and a half months he walked through the bush, alone and with other people, sometimes as many as fifty, and today he says that at the end of it he was convinced that there was one last big tree waiting to be discovered in the Wollemi gorges. It was a curious belief—the other known rare species in the mountains were mostly small plants, and new species of trees tend to be eucalypts (eight or so in the past four years). The idea of a large tree, a new genus completely unknown, growing within two hundred kilometres of Sydney, was unlikely. During and after the heritage walk, Jones inspired a group of local people, including Dave Noble, with his interest in rare species.

A few days after being given the small branch, Jones asked Noble what plant it came from. When told it was a big tree, he explained that this couldn't be right; the branch he had in his hand looked like it came from a fern. Not finding a ready indentification in the available botanical literature, he took it down to the Botanic Gardens in Sydney, where it was suggested it was from a Chinese conifer, possibly one that had been grown in a garden in the mountains. A fortnight later, Noble and Jones went back to the site and collected some more specimen material, and took some video footage. It's an indication of the ruggedness of the area that they got lost, and only reached the site on dusk. Jones realised that in the early 1980s he had walked down this very valley himself, while doing a flora survey, and must have passed within one hundred metres of one of the pines.

Back home, Jones asked Jan Allen, a botanist who had

done some voluntary work with him earlier, to help him identify the material. Allen lives at the Botanic Gardens at Mount Tomah, which has a good collection of small conifers, and there are many mature trees in gardens in the area. They looked at living species and went through the literature and realised they needed more material. On another visit to the site, a small female cone was obtained, which was cut open on a breadboard in Jan Allen's kitchen one night. The interior design of the cone, plus other characteristics already noted, indicated that a new genus had been found, and the discoverers opened a bottle of champagne.

Jones and Allen then decided to publish a paper on the new genus, and to keep it a secret until the paper was ready. They wanted the intellectual challenge, and the personal satisfaction, of naming the genus after Dave Noble and of presenting their find to the world by way of a scientific paper in the Royal Botanic Gardens' journal *Telopea*. Also, they were concerned about the safety of the pine. They worked through the nights for three weeks and then asked Ken Hill, a senior botanist at the Botanic Gardens and an expert on conifers, to assist with the taxonomic description. Hill agreed that Dave Noble had found a new genus. The term *genus*, as used in taxonomy, is part of a *family*, and usually consists of more than one *species*. In this case the genus *Wollemia* contains only one species, *Wollemia nobilis*.

The acceptance of the discovery by the scientific community brought with it the need to work out what to do next. The Wollemi Pine Recovery Committee, involving officers from N.P.W.S. and the Royal Botanic Gardens, was set up, and later evolved into the Joint Conservation Team, headed by Bob Conroy, the manager of the Central Region of N.P.W.S. The first priorities were to find out how many of the pines were in existence, and where they were, and to stop people from visiting them. A search was launched, by air and on foot, of the Wollemi National park. A smaller group of pines was found about a kilometre upstream from the first. Between them the sites contained fewer than forty adult trees, and a number of seedlings. And that is it. According to Bob Conroy, "We're 99 per cent sure there are no more sites out there. We've studied lots of aerial photographs, and once you know what you're looking for the pine is remarkably distinctive, given its size and colour. We can't see any more."

The main element in protecting the pines has been secrecy. Very few people know exactly where they are, and fewer have actually seen them. People living near the access road nearest the sites have been asked to report any cars using the road immediately, and Bob Conroy is fairly confident that no unauthorized visitors have reached the pines (despite news reports to the contrary). His officers have given talks to schools and other groups around the area, to explain the importance of protecting the pine. More generally, N.P.W.S. have made information, including videos and photographs, available to the media and the public, and have even allowed a commercial film crew to visit the site to film the pines for the IMAX film at The Edge cinema at Katoomba. Seedlings have been displayed at the Royal Botanic Gardens, and the public has been told that it will be able to buy seedlings in a few years. The purpose of all this has been to reduce the air of mystery and rarity surrounding the pines, thereby reducing the motivation of anyone—be they vandals, bushwalkers, or seed collectors—to visit the sites.

The next step was to learn more about the pine. Ken Hill has been looking at where it fits in to our knowledge of the evolution of plants and trees. It seems that the Wollemi pine represents an evolutionary line that goes back some 100 million years and was thought to have died out. There are no known fossils of the Wollemi pine but there are fossils of species from which it might have evolved. Scientists also know about a very similar pollen that existed ninety-four million years ago. *Wollemia* is a member of the conifer family *Araucariaceae*, previously thought to have just two living genera. The family was named after the region where the first species, the Monkey Puzzle Tree, was found in South America. The other Australian species of the family are the Hoop Pine,

Norfolk Island Pine, Bunya Pine and the Australian Kauri. The family was common all over the world until about 65 million years ago, when it became extinct in the northern hemisphere. It was still very common in the forests of Gondwana but gradually it was replaced by the more successful flowering plants.

Being a conifer, *Wollemia* has no flowers. It is bisexual and each tree has both female and male reproductive cones on its upper branches. (A helicopter had to be used to obtain the cones used to identify the tree.) The cones are green when young and red-brown when mature. The seeds (between ten and twenty in each cone so far examined) have "wings" and are presumably dispersed by the wind.

Rod Peakall, lecturer in conservation biology and genetics at the Australian National University, has been examining the DNA sequences of the pine, looking at specimens from six trees at one site and one at the other. Using the most advanced DNA "fingerprinting" techniques—unavailable five years ago—he has so far found no variation among the seven individuals he's looked at, which he describes as "very unusual". Two possibilities are that the trees are clones, or that they have been inbreeding for so long that genetic differences have disappeared. He is now (February 1997) about to begin the research that will determine which of these is the case.

Perhaps the greatest mystery of the pine is how this tiny population of a once common Gondwanaland tree survived in just two places in the sandstone labyrinths of Wollemi. Ken Hill says there are a thousand other gorges in the area apparently providing the same environment as the one in which the pine was found. Some people have suggested that fire played a role in the pine's survival, but charred stumps indicate that intense fire has passed through this valley just like others. So far, there seems to be nothing unique or even unusual that can be pointed to as a reason for the pine's survival. Perhaps we will never know the reason. Cathy Offord, the horticultural research officer at the Royal Botanic Gardens, Mount Annan, has written that the pines might simply be the last survivors of a dying species. There might be no particular reason (beyond a string of minute happenings in the past) why they are where they are rather than somewhere else in the area.

Another curiosity is that, for such a rare tree, it seems to grow fairly easily when cultivated. Since early 1995 Cathy Offord has been involved in growing about five hundred seedlings from cuttings and seeds. She now believes the pine will grow well in Sydney gardens—indeed, it appears that, like the Bunya and the Norfolk Pines, it is hardy enough to grow in many places around the world. When cultivated it should take three to four years for a small seedling to reach the height of a big Christmas tree. Tenders have been called from plant nurseries interested in cultivating and selling the pine. According to the Joint Preservation Team's Bob Conroy, the trademark name Jurassic Pine has been registered. They are having difficulties with the preferred phrase Wollemi Pine, as it is considered too "generic". (That is, too close to its common name.) Money made from the sale of the pine will go to the research and preservation of the Wollemi pine and other rare species.

Cultivation involves a great deal more than just sticking a cutting in a test tube. The amount of knowledge needed to grow the plant successfully is considerable. Scientists at the Royal Botanic Gardens and the University of Sydney are examining the mycorrhizal associations between fungi living in the soil and the roots of the trees. These associations are symbiotic and increase a plant's capacity to take up nutrients from the soil—a particularly necessary gift for Australian native plants, given the poor nutritional quality of much of our soil. The scientists need to find out how important such fungi will be to the pine's success as a cultivated tree. They have discovered that fungi on the tree's foliage can process taxol, which could be a cancer-controlling drug, although taxol is not rare.

The most important purpose of cultivation so far, though, has been to ensure the existence of a population of the pine "ex situ" (away from its natural site) in case the trees in the wild are destroyed by fire or any other cause. In the 1950s about fifty individuals of a new species, *Eucalyptus copulans,* were found in the Blue Mountains. The species did not fare well, and in 1996 the only known surviving example in the wild was knocked over in a storm. Mount Annan, however, holds two individual trees, which could now be reintroduced into the wild.

It is conceivable that the wild populations of the Wollemi pine will not survive their discovery. Part of the tree's root system, for example, is close to the surface and is being trodden on and compressed by everyone who visits the site, despite their best intentions. Another risk is the introduction of pathogenic fungi on the clothes or shoes of visitors (although steps are being taken by the current, authorised visitors, to prevent this from happening). It is not yet known what the results of all this might be—it is possible, of course, that the trees will be generally unaffected.

According to Bob Conroy, spreading the trees to other parts of the wilderness is not an option, at least not for the moment. There seems to be a feeling that where the trees were found is essential to what they mean to us, and to scatter them throughout the national park—were this possible—would destroy some of this significance, as well as possibly changing their genetic makeup and affecting the ecology of other areas.

Michael Duffy

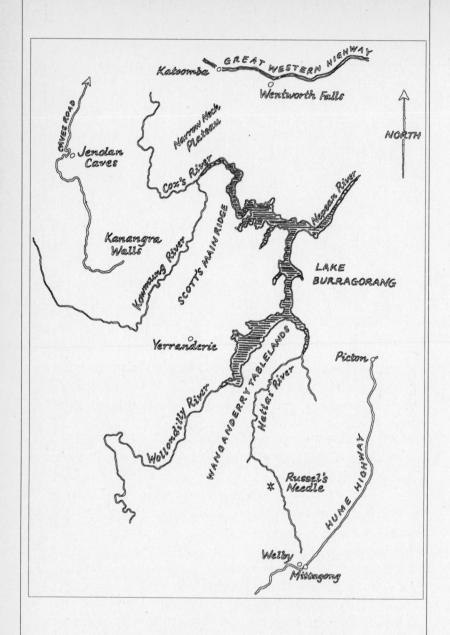

Map 3: SOUTHERN BLUE MOUNTAINS
showing general location of David Foster's walk

XII

David Foster

A Walk in the Southern Blue Mountains

D avid Foster was born in Katoomba and his first novel,
The Pure Land, is partly set there. Today he lives in
Bundanoon which is in the Southern Highlands,
much of which area, he argues below, forms the southern
extremity of the Blue Mountains. Foster has spent a considerable amount of time in the bush of this region. In late 1996
he walked from near Mittagong to Katoomba, partly by way
of the Barrallier track. What follows is an account of this trip,
and a reflection on wilderness and the experience of being a
white person in the Australian bush.

The New South Wales Blue Mountains appear, on a fine day,
blue because of oil droplets in the leaves of the eucalypts that
push the green of the chlorophyll molecules in the eucalypt
leaves towards the blue end of the spectrum. This effect is not
confined to eucalypts. Walking in Turkey in 1993 I was struck
by how blue the pine-covered mountains of the Ida Range
appeared when I could see them through the smog that blew

across Gallipoli from Europe. Blue mountains, precisely because of the organic exhalations that render them blue, are
flammable mountains, burning, when they burn, fiercely, in
periods of high temperature and low humidity. They are pleasant to look at, but dangerous to live upon.

By late November it can be too hot to walk with
comfort in the Blue Mountains. You daren't light a fire, in
time of total fire ban, to cook your tucker and sterilise your
tea. Campers shit along the watercourses. Chlorine tablets
don't work on giardia parasites and a dehydrating bout of
diarrhoea can be worse than a load of blisters. Early November, despite the vagaries of Spring, can be a good time to
walk in the mountains, if like me, you are drawn by the song
of the whistlers (rufous and golden) along those same watercourses.

The Blue Mountains, seen across the Cumberland
Plain from the colony of Sydney, formed, providentially, a
barricade to the wandering mobs of cattle decamping from
the colony. These mobs, a valuable resource, along with the
men of mostly Irish and convict extraction who depastured
and rustled them, form a significant chapter in the European
history of the southern Blue Mountains. They haunt the place
still. In April 1996 a walker was attacked by a feral bull at the
conflux of Kowmung River and Ti Willa Creek. So sheer, it
is more properly sheep country, but the dingoes made it im-
practical to run sheep. The dingoes are still out there. Two
days back I disturbed five dingoes as I drove at dawn in my
Landrover down the old Oberon Colong stock route. Big
red handsome dingoes, within a hundred kilometres of
Sydney's CBD.

The port of Sydney was established east of one of the
most intractable massifs in the whole Great Divide. Kanangra
Tops and the Murruin Plateau, either side of the upper
Kowmung Gorge, rise to over four thousand feet. Fifteen
minutes into a flight from Sydney to Perth and watch the
passengers' eyes drift from the windows. West of the Blue
Mountains, Australia is all but featureless to the shores of the
Indian Ocean.

It soon became apparent that despite their relatively unimposing altitude the Blue Mountains were a real barrier. An intrepid emancipated convict named Wilson reappeared in Sydney wearing a kangaroo skin after venturing up the Wollondilly perhaps as far as what is now Goulburn in 1798, and no doubt the odd scrub bull made it through to the west, but it was twenty-five years after settlement before the first official crossing. Today, two centuries later, we still underestimate the Blue Mountains. In the first week of November 1996, the month in which I am walking and writing, thirteen schoolboys were winched from the Grose Valley by Careflight helicopter and taken to Katoomba Hospital. They were suffering burns, from an exploding gas bottle, and hypothermia. They should have been in their tents in their sleeping bags waiting for the weather to clear. The temperature on my place at Bundanoon that morning was four degrees C. I could see my breath as I milked the cow. In such Macquarie Island weather, bush walking in the Blue Mountains becomes a misery. If you've no dry clothes and your sleeping bag's wet you can die of exposure. Eucalypt leaves depend vertically, so give you little shelter from the rain. They don't give you much shade from the sun or protection from the wind for the same reason. Big dead limbs break off them in a wind. They're not really friends of ours.

I was born in Katoomba fifty-three years ago, when the postman still delivered the mail by horse. These mountains are nowhere much more than four thousand feet high, but very ancient, gently uplifted, scarcely tilted, weathered and flattened. They feel more like a weathered plateau than a mountain range as such. But while only patches today remain of the forests of the Mediterranean, and those of California and Chile and south Africa's Cape Province are mostly scrub, the Blue Mountains boast the finest example on the planet of a dry, evergreen forest. Stand at Echo Point and you will see, beyond the Three Sisters, towards Mittagong, a Wilderness of dry sclerophyll forest, broken only by the faces of sandstone and shale too sheer for vegetation, and here and there, on an east facing wall, by the richer green of a warm temperate rainforest along a watercourse. This is a landscape in which most species have names only white botanists ever knew and no-one, in my view, black or white, has ever fully possessed it.

Much of the intractability of these mountains has to do with extremes of weather. Ten days ago I was walking Scott's Main Range in thirty-five-degree heat. Yesterday snow was falling in Oberon. I recall a two-day walk I undertook two years back, also in November, two days of terrific heat, in the Mount Armour region of Kanangra-Boyd. It was so hot on the ridges that, because no water was to be had, I could not hydrate myself sufficiently. Walking those ridges of sand and stone was like walking a desert in Palestine. I sweat so freely at thirty-five Celsius I cannot compensate for the sweat I lose and cramp up in the calves at night. But I venture out there partly to recall what it is to be tired, thirsty, hungry and dirty, the better to appreciate a European bed, Coca Cola, pizza and hot showers. When I got back to my motorcycle, the air changed as an ominous cloud bank suddenly appeared to the south. I knew I had to get out of there fast. If I didn't I could be there for days. So I slid and slipped down Yerranderie Track in the rain and the sleet with the headlight on, dodging falling timber. By the time I reached Taralga I was so cold I couldn't undo my petrol cap to refuel. Couldn't get my wallet out of my jacket to pay. Far from cramping up with heat exhaustion I was shivering uncontrollably. Had I dropped the bike on the road I doubt I would have been able to lift it. I doubt I would have been able to light a fire or construct a sensible shelter. It's at times like these, when a mistake could be fatal, you appreciate the discipline of Wilderness. It can focus the mind and by focusing your mind it produces, paradoxically, a sense of relaxation, but that's later. You can't afford to shiver on a bike or you lose control of the bike.

I prefer to be alone and I believe a white man can be more alone in the Blue Mountains than almost anyplace, because we European settlers don't as yet have eucalypt dreaming. I have oak dreaming. A spell of walking in Ireland's Wicklow and Kerry National Park three months back has left me in no doubt of it. When I was a boy looking out of my window at the Astor Flats in Katoomba Street, over the present-day National Bank, I could see beyond the Cecil Guesthouse a plateau verdant in Spring with English oak and Monterey pine. Beyond, as far as I could see, was eucalypt forest. And this has not changed, whatever else has.

What is the extent of the Blue Mountains? In the beginning they were just the mountains the citizens of Sydney could see to their west. If we define them as the range of the rock warbler—he's the little brown guy hops along the vertical face of a cliff going 'pink pink pink'—they are geologically the hinterland of Hawkesbury and Narrabeen Sandstone with adjacent outcrops of limestone. This definition would encompass the Bundanoon Sector of the Morton Park near where I live, but to get to Mittagong from Bundanoon Gorge entails a walk over thirty kilometres of mostly cleared basalt farmland. Certainly, what I see from my window reminds me of what I saw as a boy. A gorge of Hawkesbury Sandstone. Rice flowers, *Pimelia thymifolia*. Messmate stringybark, *Eucalyptus obliqua*. Mountain devils, *Lambertia formosa*, one of the many proteas that typify the Blue Mountains. Mind you, I've seen mountain devils at sea level in the Royal National Park. When I was a kid we made infernal bodies for their devil seed heads, from pipe cleaners.

Alternatively, we could define the Blue Mountains as the eastern sector of the Great Divide that lies within the Central Tableland of N.S.W. This would take us from somewhere near Crookwell to somewhere on the Putty Road, but Crookwell is open grazing country and we prefer our Blue Mountains to be Wilderness, so let us propose an area extending from, say, Goodman's Crossing on the Wollondilly River near Wombeyan Caves (explored by Wilson—the Bush Fire Brigade down there still got the old Studebaker Six Wheel Drive but don't bring it to town)—and the Upper Nattai Gorge in the Nattai National Park to the south—that's the wooded gorge you see from the Big Dipper on the Mittagong

Bypass as you scoot down the Hume—to Wollemi National
Park in the north. This would include the Warragamba Catchment to the south, Newnes and the Wolgan Valley to the
north, with the Blue Mountains and Kanangra-Boyd
National Parks as the indisputable core. Conservationists pressing for a Greater Blue Mountains National Park would argue
for this definition, but not all of it is Wilderness.

   I have walked sections of the Kerry Way, the Wicklow
Way, the Cotswold Way, the St Kilda ridgewalk beyond the
Outer Hebrides— troubled, on the last, by a fog so thick I
couldn't read a compass at one point—and all walking is delightful, even if walking in Europe or Anatolia is rural rather
than wilderness walking. *Solvitur ambulando*: a solution lies in
walking. In Turkey you meet with shepherds and peasants, in
Ireland with Euroteens. Any rural walk is fine by me, as solitary walking is a meditation besides being the best exercise
there is: I count sixty thousand footsteps plus in a ten-hour
hike. It doesn't hurt your back, like running does. I like to
identify plants as I walk but I don't walk for the purpose of
identifying plants. I no longer seek a physical challenge: indeed, I had knee surgery in June. Like many a middle-aged
westerner I walk because I am so depressed I doubt I want to
go on living. And I find that being alone in the bush eases
this existential pain. I find that being alone with Nature always eases egotistical pain. The agnostic can understand the
concept of a pilgrimage, because the walk is a metaphor for
life itself. You start the day bright and fresh but come three
pm you feel as though you've been trudging along for fifty-
three years.

   What will become of Civilized Man when Nature no
longer exists? We know what becomes of Civilized Man when
God no longer exists. I've seen it said depressive illness will
be a major human affliction, on a par with cardiac illness and
cancer, by the year 2020. I can believe that. Wilderness is the
Reset Button. No Wilderness, no Reset.

In a sense there is no longer Wilderness. There is only comparative Wilderness now. As a deckhand on trawlers in the

tropics I find no cay not littered with netting and plastics. The closest wild places to which I have access are the Ettrema Gorge in the Morton Park—the horizon from my window is Ettrema Plateau—and the Kowmung in the Kanangra-Boyd Park, that gorge between the snow gum and hop bitter pea country of Mt Werong/Mt Shivering, Jenolan Caves and the Tonalli Range. They are both declared wildernesses or soon will be. I can get to either in a day of dirt driving, but anywhere I pitch my swag I'm watching satellites overhead, and the Kowmung lies under a major flightpath. Planes pass over night and day. More pertinently, there is nowhere I can go where others haven't been before me. To my chagrin no plant is named after me. Men like Myles Dunphy (with swag and rifle), Paddy Pallin (pack but no rifle) mapped and named the wild country round Sydney, purely for the sake of so doing. This was not that long ago, earlier this century, but human population has more than doubled since then. Cattlemen, miners and cedarcutters, intent on making fortunes, were there before the Pallins and the Dunphys, but these tended to keep their knowledge to themselves, as wise businessmen will. What they knew we don't know. In country 'absolutely unknown to the masses' as Dunphy put it in his 1914 diary, he encountered cattlemen's huts, mullock heaps, even bags of spuds.

The Blue Mountains were ever a sanctuary for thieves and outcasts, both black and white. The Aborigines encountered by Barrallier in his several sorties across the Burragorang Valley appear to have included tribal outcasts lacking the numbers to hunt 'roo. The bushrangers Starlight and Butcher are recalled in Starlight's Trail on the Nattai and Butcher's Creek below Scott's Main Range. The Irish New Country with its myriad little churches stretches down the open western Slopes from Mudgee to Booroowa. It's a great sight to the petty cattleman and beekeeper in November, the grass tall and the Curse in flower. Many a rogue found attractive the prospect of duffing cattle in Bathurst or Goulburn, driving them through the Burragorang Valley and selling them in Camden. There is still the odd scrub bull about, not to mention pigs and goats, some regrowth cedar on Carlon's Creek, Wonga Wonga Brook. Gold fossickers found nothing to speak of, but the ghost town of Yerranderie, with the ruins of its Silver Peak silver mine, is worth a look. Good base for a walk. There were two thousand people living in Yerranderie between 1890 and 1900. Last week there was just Dave the caretaker and me. Dave's another Blue Mountain boy, Valley Heights. Like Michael, who does a bit of carpentry there, owns a hundred acres at Mt Colong would take time to sell, Dave got an old Landrover and a BMW Boxer Twin. But on the whole I believe life remote in the High Country tends to promote a certain individualism.

'Michael's got some funny ideas,' confides Dave. 'I won't say they're wrong.'

I bet a quid they're not wrong.

What constitutes Wilderness? Let's give it a capital. My Webster's Dictionary defines it as 'a pathless waste of any kind'. In an address given in 1965 Dr J. Mosley, then Director of the Australian Conservation Foundation, remarked, 'One of the chief characteristics of wilderness recreation is that it is confined. If the country within the reserve is to invite the visitor to wander where he will and present a challenge to route-finding skills, it must be kept as wild as possible. The landscape should exude an atmosphere of countless freedom. Any attempt to influence movement is clearly incompatible and these areas should be kept trackless, hutless and bridgeless. Roads and graded tracks obviously have no place in such an area. However, there is a difference of opinion among wilderness users about the desirability of having marked routes. I believe an element of danger should be accepted as an essential ingredient of wilderness. If, in spite of this consideration, track markings and survival huts are thought necessary for safety, they should be minimal and strictly prescribed. The spontaneity of the visit can be spoiled by many things which are useful in some parts of a national park but undesirable in a wilderness area, such as warning notices, interpretive signs, uniformed rangers, entrance gates and other visitor paraphernalia which suggests to the traveller that he is entering a specially designed play area. The wilderness user can obtain all the information he needs from maps and pamphlets.'

—Quoted by the Budawang Committee, an organisation of conservationists set up to serve the Morton Park as Milo Dunphy's Colong Committee served the Kanangra-Boyd.

Do you like a track, do you like to see a track? Or do you hate, despise and abhor them. This is the crux of Wilderness. This is the crux of walking in the bush. You will have no time to listen to the birds and admire the flowers where there's no track. But, on the plus side, no track, no shit.

If I walk from where I now live—or more strictly, from my eldest daughter Sam's place at Welby near Mittagong—to where I was born, which I can do without walking through a farm or a town, I walk on tracks for the most part. These tracks range from the graded clay firetrail to the barely perceptible cairn-marked pad that requires some tracking skill to pursue. Much of the route is negotiable; a scramble down a gorge, a slog along a so-called 'river flat' overgrown with wattles and nettles, a climb up an obvious saddle or spur towards a pass. The quality of my experience is determined by whether or not I am following a track, and, if I am following a track, by the nature of the track that I am following.

When the Warragamba Dam was constructed in 1960 the lower part of the Burragorang Valley was flooded, and to protect the quality of Sydney's drinking water, farming, mining and timbergetting in the Valley were proscribed. The Warragamba Catchment, which includes the Nattai National Park (gazetted in 1991), is jointly administered by Sydney Water and the National Parks and Wildlife. They don't always see eye to eye. The Water Board don't want people walking through their Catchment, let alone camping on it, because people shit. They shit near campsites and they camp beside watercourses, making for bad water. The Water Board has built or upgraded vehicular trails throughout the Catchment, maintained, nowadays, by a single gang with a crew of three, not so long ago by five gangs each with a crew of twenty plus, so we're seeing these trails at their best. In contrast, the National Parks and Wildlife don't seem overly fussed when the firetrails it inherits become impassable and inaccessible. Firetrails attract hoons on motorcycles and horses and four-wheel-drive clubs, and eucalypt forest was born to burn, so why seek to circumvent Nature's purposes?

Today, if you want to walk in the southern Blue Mountains you can utilise the Water Board trails, though you cannot camp in the Water Board Restricted Zone. The time will surely come when walkers will be forbidden from entering Wilderness. The immuno-suppressed of the big cities, those walking Petrie dishes of microbial evolution, will see to it.

I don't walk for the purpose of testing my route-finding skills. I'm happy just to look at the flowers and listen to the birds from a formed earth road. If the presence of track annuls Wilderness, then that sense of guilt and despair at what we have done to the earth the formed earth track provokes makes me, for one, content to admire Wilderness without plunging into it and shitting on it, just to test my route-finding skills. Our own shit, of course, never offends us.

There's a two-day climbing wall in the States where you bivvy on the cliff face in the evening. The base of this cliff is a collage of toilet paper, and some ledges and some handholds are smeared with human faeces.

Wilderness is better off without us. All I ask is that I be alone at a vantage point from which to perceive it and if it's too easy to get to that point I suppose I won't be alone there. Today it is rare for me to meet another walker on the trail but I choose my times. I avoid holidays and weekends.

Wilderness doesn't change much from one human generation to the next. It certainly doesn't change at the rate that men and fashions and ambitions change. In the last years of the second millennium A.D., this is the solace of Wilderness. In Wilderness, Eternity. The sea is Wilderness too, or was. If you've been so lucky as to have lived with access to the Blue Mountains all but a few years of your life, you will therein experience forgotten memories that no human interaction can evoke. Some think it irresponsible to venture into Wilderness alone, but Wilderness is being alone. Company is chatter. If I get bitten by a tiger snake I'll wear it, because if there's one sight I never want to see it's that Careflight helicopter hovering over me.

<hr>

Some highlights of a Russel's Needle—Three Sisters traverse, mid November '96.

The longleafed waxflower, *Eriostemon myoporoides*, is in nascent bloom along the top of the Wattle Ridge. I'm out there perving on the big pink buds. Can there exist, in the whole Blue Mountains, a more attractive shrub? With its lanceolate leaves and big white flowers it makes an attractive and long-lived bouquet. A Pommy wouldn't pick it for an Aussie at all, so *Eriostemon*, like the related *Boronia* (named after the French botanist who fell to his death in trying to pick one), is deemed suitable for cultivation as an ornamental. What is this saying?

My grandfather, who walked in a waistcoat and suit, introduced me to the Blue Mountains on his shoulders. Fifty years on I question my own aesthetics. *Eriostemon*, the same family as *Citrus*, has a leaf the colour of a lemon bush. Now we of European stock crave that green. In the bush our eyes are drawn towards it. Eucalypt green is not yet a 'true' green for us. We are not yet really 'here'. I grew up in an oak grove.

In October 1988, as a bicentennial gesture—and thanks, in no small part, to the efforts of Robert Sloss of Mittagong—Mittagong was linked to Katoomba via the Ensign Barrallier Track, which is waymarked, along the Nattai River, by squares of blue sisal nailed to trees. Most walkers choose to finish the route in Mittagong. I go the other way for sentimental reasons and I choose my route depending on how I'm feeling, what the weather's like, how long I can afford to be away. I don't usually do the whole walk at once.

It's a waste of time, but like non-reproductive sex, walking never feels to be a waste of time. Two or three days is always enough to hit the Reset Button.

Sydney Water determines the route. You mustn't linger in their restricted zone. From Mittagong the walk takes you up the Nattai Valley. From Vineyard Flat on the Nattai you cross the Wanganderry Tableland via Beloon Pass and fording the Wollondilly shortly thereafter at Murphy's Flat near the Jooriland River, proceed to Yerranderie. From Yerranderie you walk up the gentle Scott's Main Range through Byrne's Gap in the Axehead Range dropping, at some ridge of your choosing, thirteen hundred feet to the Middle Kowmung. Where the Kowmung enters Cox's River you ascend, through the Wild Dog Range, to Medlow Gap, thence, via Taros Ladder, to Narrow Neck and on to Katoomba. The scenery is quite varied. You cannot easily get lost as you're mostly walking up a road or down a river, but you can take longer than you expect, especially if you strike bad weather. On 4 March 1989 Peter Treseder ran the 140 kilometres in fourteen hours. (I doubt he could do it today, given the condition of the Nattai Flats.) For lesser mortals the walk might mean a night on the Nattai, a night on the Tonalli at Yerranderie, a night on the Kowmung, a night on the Cox's River. You could travel light if they'd let you take in an axe and a rifle, but they won't.

I go down Starlight's Track to avoid walking the Lower Nattai Gorge, thus saving myself two days of the most difficult walking on the whole route. No one, I suspect, who has walked the Lower Gorge will scruple thereafter to avoid it. The Upper Gorge in contrast is not hard to get at and a pleasant day walk from Mittagong. I did it on a weekend this November as a round trip from my daughter's place in Welby. I walked down Box Vale Track and back up Gibbergunyah Creek through the river peppermints, *Eucalyptus elata*, under the freeway. The Box Vale Track, which is on Crown Land, was reopened in 1986 by the Lands Department.

It was the first fine day after the cold wet weather saw the schoolboys lifted out of the Grose. The silver-top ash was in flower as I have never seen it flower in twenty years. The lower ridges by the freeway from the track looked as though dusted with a tin of talc. What a pity my bees work it for pollen rather than nectar, I thought. But they were on a clover flow. I went down the track through the cuttings, along the embankments, on the old tramway. It's a pleasant five-kilometre stroll to the box-car loading area, coal still on the ground there. You lower yourself with the aid of a steel cable down to the Box Vale Creek junction. There are bellbirds in the Box Vale Creek, they never seem to stray far. They are so localised you could construct a bellbird map of the Blue Mountains, a bellbird songline.

Within forty minutes of setting out I was conscious of a mood lift; initial weather and initial route are so important, and it helps to have been born in the right place. I soon heard the antiphonal call of the spotted pardalote, a choked ride cymbal, ballad slow.

'*Tweet tidit*'
'*Tweet tidit*'

The female answers the male in the manner of the whip bird. A descending trill from a fan-tailed cuckoo, the hoot of a wonga pigeon, the pardalote's antiphonal hesitant, persistent—these to me are the sounds of the Mountains in Spring that prime my Reset Button. And which flowers do you suppose were doing well? Each year a particular floral species does particularly well, so spring is never the same twice, but you need to walk for many years before this starts to register. This year it was silver-top ash, a middling eucalypt found on poor sandy soil. It has a rough stocking like a red bloodwood, not so tessellated. Beautiful leaves though, most delightful in winter gales, when they shine in the sun. You can see silver-top ash, *Eucalyptus sieberi*, all the way up from the Wollongong scarp. It is always accompanied by the summer- or fall-flowering scribbly gum, *Eucalyptus racemosa*, hereabouts. Silver-top ash looks nothing like a European ash. We have to plant our claret ashes.

Nodding blue lily, *Stypandra glauca*, was doing well on the black shale soil of the Box Vale, along with mountain dampiera, *Dampiera purpurea*. I don't recall ever seeing mountain dampiera here before. But this year I found it in flower all down the Nattai and over the Wanganderry Walls to the Wollondilly. A small plant with a brilliant dark blue flower, almost a cobalt blue. Waratahs, *Telopea speciosissima*, were flowering on the Box Vale Track the other side of the tunnel, within earshot of the freeway. It's been a good year for waratahs. You mainly see them round Mittagong. People pick them and cattle eat them, so they're rare in the Blue Mountains today.

If I turned right at the river I could walk up Claude Lee Pass through the Sydney blue gum and coast white box, *Eucalypti saligna* and *quadrangulata*, to the Upper Gorge. Claude Lee Pass, named after the poet and shire clerk of Mittagong, is well worn in, a pleasant walk among coachwoods, *Ceratopetalum apetalum*, along the blacksoil banks of the river. The Upper Nattai is infested with buttercups and the waters here are turbid but the golden whistlers were singing.

'Chee chee chee chee chee chee chee tu whit'

Had I turned left at the Nattai the going would have been harder. In theory the way is marked but in practice the marks are hard to find and the frequently fern-covered track is not worn in all the way down to Round Flat, where you hit the Nattai Road. You scramble along, seeking the best route you can, for two days, and you don't have time to notice things, beyond where to put your feet. You need to keep vigilant. I knew I'd be doing my scrambling later on the lower flats, so I didn't feel guilty. But there is one feature of the Lower Gorge I did need to see. I needed to walk in down Starlight's Track, then back upriver to Needle Creek. Everyone knows the Three Sisters but few have seen the Fourth. She stands alone in the Wilderness of the Lower Nattai Gorge where She goes under the name of 'Russel's Needle'.

I carry in my mind a view of Her which I didn't get from the banks of the Nattai. You want to get above a needle. There's a track goes in from High Range on the Wombeyan Caves Road brings you out on what's marked on the map as a helipad. I wouldn't like to try to land a helicopter there. I went in although I knew it meant driving through a gate marked 'Private Property' because if there's one thing gets to me it's landholders putting gates on firetrails. When I'm driving the Bushfire tanker I'll happily take them off their hinges. When you walk in Ireland or Turkey you're free to walk anywhere, even a public road. Mount Flora property at Colo Vale has the only road access to the Upper Nattai, and they've seen fit to erect, not just a locked gate over the road, but the picture of a walker wearing a red diagonal. Dogs, bikes, cars, fair enough, but what harm can a walker do? We need more shepherds here and fewer fences.

I soon had company. A man with a great view of Mount Jellore from his front door, in his towelling hat with his working dogs on the tabletop. He explained how the land was his private property. I explained how the road across his property was a public road, but I knew he'd have backup from the Parks and Wildlife because they don't want people in there either. We decided I could go in just the once, because I'm an officer of the Bush Fire Brigade. I drove, just the once, through to the Nattai, above Mount Jellore. It's Wilderness, you can't take vehicles in there now. There's a sign to that effect but there's also a private house down there, the kind that tends to be occupied by some anti-social Yugoslav with a couple of big dogs, plopped on what was at one time cleared land, now covered in wombats, nodding blue lily and broad-leafed hickory, *Acacia falciformis*. I left the Landrover ten kilometres from the Gorge, above the house, and walked in. It was getting late.

I reached the Gorge, about a thousand-foot drop, at five thirty pm. There were storms about, but being blown seaward by strong westerly winds. These promptly dropped at dusk, as they do when you're trying to get a fire going before the missus comes home from work. Against the backlight the November sun was strong and sharp, producing wonderful chiaroscuro. Russel's Needle stood centre stage encircled by mountains and cliffs. I could see downriver to Starlight's Hollow. I could see the Nattai below, winding its way through the big sheoaks, *Casuarina cunninghamiana*. I could see upriver the cleared slopes of Mount Flora. I shall never forget that view. The Needle stands maybe two hundred metres out into the Valley, looking like the middle of the Three Sisters or one of those Apostles off the Victorian Coast, an exposed buttress on a sandstone head where the connecting rock has weathered away. There are eucalypts growing on the top of the Needle as there are on the Three Sisters. This was a view of Wilderness, certainly; breathtaking, difficult, if not illegal, of access, unmistakable for anywhere else, vulnerable, like sandstone. How long can a sandstone needle persist?

You can also see Russel's Needle from Needle Creek where the Nattai debouches from the Lower Gorge. Just an occasional glimpse through the sheoaks but put these two perspectives together and you have a subject for thought on your walk. The Fourth Sister flees from the other Three in the Jamison Valley and now has absolute privacy, while They have the floodlights.

Starlight's Track follows Starlight's Creek to the Nattai from Wattle Ridge. We're told the bushranger Starlight used this track but that could be apocryphal. There's *Coopernookia barbata* here—love the name of that taxon—an uncommon pea, *Bossiaea neo-anglica*, and here you get your first glimpse of the tall willowy cedar wattle, *Acacia elata*, and the monstrous fern leafed spider flower, *Grevillea longifolia*. I think of these as Blue Mountain species, I've not seen them in the Morton Park. There's cedar wattle in Bundanoon, but introduced. From Box Vale Creek to Round Flat, a distance of some thirty kilometres, the waymarked Ensign Barrallier track is all but impossible to find. The Nattai here is up to ten metres wide but often only centimetres deep. There are ducks, mostly black, on the river, and water monitors that dive like platypus. But the fauna you are most likely to see are the black snakes, with which the Nattai is infested. Mostly they stand their ground but sometimes they'll head for the water when disturbed, and move through the water with the selfsame motion they use to move across sand. You can't help but admire them. No-one ever died from a black snake bite and they're easy to see on the rocks where they bask, but I went close to treading on a copperhead once, so I keep my eyes to the ground. You need to, because the ubiquitous snakes, the wombat burrows, the flood debris, the slippery stones at river crossings, the ferns, the dead and broken wattle boughs, and most annoyingly, those nettles—all these render walking the Nattai 'Flats' an exhausting trial of patience. The Fourth Sister would have been tired and scratched and perhaps lost by the time she got to Starlight's. I find it less tiring to ignore the waymarks, on the rare occasions I see one, reconciling myself to a negotiable slog, and I suspect others do the same. Which is why the track is not worn in. The Nattai Flats, where cattle grazed for a century, are reverting to bush. Personally, I find it dispiriting to see former pasture in such a condition.

Where you have no track to follow you can only relax at the campsite, and you never fully relax on a walk like this when you are alone. I am more afraid of getting lost than hurt, though I'm more likely to get hurt than lost. That part of me wants out sits there, tingling with nettle stings, forcing down some horrible camp tucker. Barrallier reports the river 'teeming with fish of various species, especially black bream, of four to six pounds.' Those were the days. There were swamps back then, teeming with eels. So the blacks and the cattle duffers ate well, though Barrallier carried flour and pickled pork, which ran out after only three days. They must have been hoeing into it.

First night out for me is a time of intense despondency. I feel adrift at dusk, apprehensive without the bustle of my normal domestic routine. But I don't feel afraid when darkness falls because there is nothing to fear. There are no bears, there are no big cats, and though Hilltop is Milat country, I can't see Milat stalking on foot. He'd be on his trail bike, for sure. As I lie back watching the stars and satellites I fall asleep with a sense of gratitude and a strange longing for what surrounds me, a longing, like the wistful longing of the wild dingo for human contact, to be indulged, rather than assuaged.

I doze off thinking of a beautiful sassafras, *Doryphora*

sassafras, I found, as a steeple of rainforest green on the oaky river bank. We apply the name 'oak' to the casuarina, so desperate are we to say the word. I can't pass a sassafras without I crush a handful of the green serrated leaves to savour their redolence. I do that with bog myrtle in Ireland too.

I like to be walking by dawn in fine weather, just to hear the dawn chorus. I don't have to speak to a soul. How can I be a gloomy fellow when the big-balled blue wren is bursting with such song? The shadows are softer at the hour of dawn, the bush less masculine. A principal benefit of camping out is to be up and about at dawn. The spotted pardalotes are back in song and the bellbirds in Travis Gully too. But you can hear bellbirds on the upper Nattai Road if you want an easy entry to the Nattai.

The traverse from the Nattai to the Wollondilly over the Wanganderry Tableland takes about four hours and involves a steep two hundred metre descent down the Wanganderry Walls. These Walls, which extend over twenty kilometres along the eastern bank of the Wollondilly, are broken and timbered at the dip of Beloon Pass, where the scree has formed an easy ladder to the ten-metre-wide and five-metre-deep break in the cliff face. The Fourth Sister would have come up this pass, perhaps pursued by anthropophagi intent upon torture, rape, murder and exploration. There's a red toolbox at the top of the pass with a book in it for wayfarers to sign. Judging by the dates in this book, about a party a week goes up Beloon Pass. I'd had a fall and hurt my back in Travis Gully so I was glad of a spell to sit and read. A cool westerly wind was blowing hard from the Twin Peaks area to the west. If I looked up, I looked over yellow flowering apple, *Angophora bakeri*, on the scree. A wedge-tailed eagle cruised by. I am entering Blue Mountains National Park.

Jocular. 'Will now continue search for giant antediluvian whistling wombat.'

Irate. '"Delightful grassy meadows along the Nattai"— I don't think so! "well worn cattle tracks" BULLSHIT! I think Sloss should walk the track again, instead of ten years ago.'

Poignant. Twenty-first of October, from the

Springwood Bushwalkers' Club. 'We have made it! So far, so good.'

cf *Sydney Morning Herald*, 24 October. 'A 35-year-old Springwood man was airlifted from the remote Nattai Valley in the Blue Mountains yesterday after his new hiking boots blistered his feet so badly he could not walk. An NRMA Careflight Helicopter spokesman said the man was on the sixth day of a trek when his feet became badly swollen.' The Fourth Sister preserves Her modesty.

Murphy's Flat looks to me like it must have looked in the Dreaming. A huge expanse of grass dotted with eastern grey 'roos. Hereabouts, the golden whistler yields to the rufous whistler.

'*Ee chong joey joey joey*'

Barrallier's party passed by these flats. So did Wilson. Barrallier describes 'apple trees'. There is rough-barked apple here, *Angophora floribunda*. Barrallier remarks on a pink flowering ti-tree by the river. There was white flowering paperbark ti-tree, *Leptospermum attenuatum*, aplenty but the only pink flowering ti-tree I noted was the lovely Shoalhaven ti-tree, *Leptospermum rotundifolium*, and that was on a dry ridge up at Breakfast Creek. I doubt this could have been Barrallier's species.

Barrallier says he saw 'a pigeon, of the same species as those near Sydney'. This could have been Wonga pigeon, as shot and eaten by Myles Dunphy.

Barrallier says 'I heard a noise which I mistook for the lowing of several oxen, but I was undeceived in learning it was the croak of frogs of a tremendous size which were in the pond.' Southern bell frogs? These can sound like bunyips.

He says, 'I killed a small and very pretty bird. The head, the neck and part of its body were red. I shot several of them, which pleased me very much.' This sounds like crimson honeyeater. I have never seen one.

He says, 'One of them had wounded a black cockatoo, having the head and tail of a yellow colour, with black spots.' The common Blue Mountain yellow-tailed black. Always on the Monterey pinecones. But I saw a cockatoo I'd not seen before on the way to Yerranderie, the glossy black, which has no crest and makes a mewling sound. I disturbed a small family group in some casuarinas. They're uncommon, so despite the wind and the soreness in my back I fell asleep in a good mood at Yerranderie. Why should it matter how many species of birds I see in this life? I don't know.

I woke before dawn to a rip-roaring westerly gale, thinking again of Barrallier. He put a mark on his sketch of the Tonalli Range near Yerranderie, with the reference 'there I heard the surges sound'. At once I understood what he meant. First one stand, then another, of eucalypt trees roared in the gale like a sea in a tempest. These aural 'surges' are as localised as the bellbirds. You could draw a surge songline of the Blue Mountains. How The Fourth Sister must have trembled as She fled if the westerlies were blowing. I'm seeing Her now as a beautiful lubra, but her pursuers are men black and white, and I'm one of them.

Byrne's Gap in the Axehead Range is an hour's walk from Yerranderie. I stop to admire some pale blue fairy fan flowers, *Scaevola aemula*, marvelling at the imagination that construed, in the outstretched petals of *Scaevola*, the Roman soldier who held his hand in the fire to prove his courage. I climb Gander Head up a pretty gully where the blackwattle, *Callicoma serratifolia*, is starting to burst with golden balls— they make a great display as you drive down Megalong Valley from Blackheath. They're not acacias, belong to the same family as Christmas bush, *Ceratopetalum gummiferum*, which is also growing here, and coachwood. It's 'wattle' as in wattle-and-daub. Used by miners for building hut walls.

The view to the west from Gander Head. On 25 November 1802, Barrallier's journal says, of a report from his redcoats, 'after passing the range which was in front of us we would enter an immense plain; that from the height where they were on the mountain they had caught sight of only a few hills standing here and there in this plain; and that the country in front of them had the appearance of a meadow'.

A meadow? Grassland? If Scott's Main Range was grassland then—today it is heavily timbered, with nothing by the road but patches of tick bush, *Kunzea ambigua*, covered in butterflies—that would account for the enthusiasm of early white settlers, like the Cattle Kings Lakeman and Dunn, who wintered stock from the Abercrombie and Burragorang on the Cox's and the Kowmung flats and built stock yards on Scott's Main Range, not to mention larrikins like Lannigan of the Hole, Mount Werong, described (by one Billy Russell, quoted by Jim Barrett) as 'a very wild fellow ... took great interest in other people's cattle and always did his stock work on foot, often with only a shirt on'.

Barrallier's men had failed to observe Kowmung Gorge between themselves and the Gangerang Range. And above the Gangerang Range the highlands of Kanangra Tops. I was glad to get down to that river as the day was hot and my lips were windburnt. I went down at Mount Feld off the Dennis Ridge Track, keen to get off the ridge. Had the weather been wet I may have stuck with the ridge, dropping to Cox's River via Cookem Pass at the end of the trail. Once past Yerranderie you're in the Blue Mountains proper, and the tracks have been worn in by generations of bushwalkers. There are huts about.

The Kowmung has a reputation as the wildest and most unspoilt river in New South Wales. It rises south of Jenolan Caves near Shooter's Hill, swings round in its deep upper gorge below Mount Armour and Kanangra Walls, then flows north east through its middle and lower flats to join the Cox's River, which becomes the Warragamba when joined by the Wollondilly River. The Warragamba River flows into the Nepean River, which eventually becomes the Hawkesbury.

The Kowmung water runs cool and clear over round river sandstones, cream and pink. A breeze blows down the quartzite gorge. There are kurrajongs, *Brachychiton populneum*, amid the casuarinas and yellow flowering grey myrtle, *Backhousia myrtifolia*, on the grassy bank to the east; a cliff and rainforest, with trees like sandpaper fig, *Ficus coronata*, to the west. The Wollondilly is wider and faster, but the Kowmung is the quintessential Blue Mountains stream. I cannot wait to immerse myself in its clear dark waters and as I so do, I am suddenly reminded of the selfsame impulse to which I yielded three months ago, in the clear dark waters of the Galway's River, where it runs into the Upper Lake at Killarney, through Derrycunnihy, an oakwood on pink Kerry sandstone, the Oakwood of the Arbutus Tree. Hughes, Keefe, Pearce, O'Reilly, Dunn, Fitzpatrick, McMahon, Lannigan, Quig, Donohue—I think I now better comprehend the Irish cattleman settler here, and I've tasted the rigours of his working life on this walk, but what this country can never offer the pilgrim is a Wise Man of the Oak. There were no saints here, no monasteries, no tough men of God to inspire and uplift us.

I cannot resist slaking my thirst in the sparkling waters of the Kowmung. I should have waited for my normal quart of hot sweet tea and next day I pay the price for drinking unboiled water from a Blue Mountains stream.

I will swim again at the Water Board gauging station on Cox's River, a little upriver of the Kowmung conflux. Cox's River is real bad water but I have memories of picnics at Hartley Vale fifty years back when I would spend contented hours filling my billy with the small multicoloured frogs I found under each riverstone. Each time I turned a stone midstream I found a frog beneath it. I went back there on my way out of Katoomba to see if I could find a frog and of course I couldn't, and what was worse, the rocks were covered with grey slime—made me glad I wasn't thirsty.

I believe that wise men, not bushmen, tame a Wilderness. When I visited Glendalough in Ireland's County Wicklow this year I could feel how St Kevin's love for his landscape had in some spiritual measure transformed it. I have no object of pilgrimage in the Blue Mountains. The Druidic love of Nature and the oak, not yet extinct in the Dark Age Irish, makes me suspect that a precondition for pilgrimage is lacking in the Australian bush. The most meaningful walk you could ever take lies on a track blazed by a saint. But by the same token, you must make a great mental effort to be inspired by contemporary Glendalough. You must imagine you are alone there, and not surrounded by hundreds of people, most discussing the football or television programs or love affairs as they stroll. You must imagine you have arrived there after an arduous physical journey, and not by stepping off a coach that picked you up in Central Dublin that morning.

A Water Board trail ascends from the gauging station through the Wild Dogs to Medlow Gap. I took a last view of the Kowmung River, as the trail swung round to White Dog Creek. There are some beautiful trees on the White Dog Creek. Blue Mountain blue gum, *Eucalyptus deanei*, so tall and white and straight; Sydney red gum, *Angophora costata*, so tall and red and dimpled; turpentine, *Syncarpia glomerulifera*. Trees to make a logger's mouth water. Must be pushing two hundred foot. The tallest flowering plant in the mountains is a blue gum somewhere near Woodford. Goannas on the turpentines, four-foot lace monitors. They can get their claws into the turpentine bark. And where the track levels, a tall old-growth forest of messmate and mountain grey gum, *Eucalypti obliqua* and *cypellocarpa*, species they can't keep their paws off on the Errinundra Plateau in far east Gippsland. It breaks your heart to see the size of the trees they pull out of the coupes there.

Which is why we have National Parks. The loggers are fine mountain boys and the greenies urban riffraff, but the greenies are right and the loggers are wrong, ay. Nothing can change till men start to worship trees again, as St Kevin did. Christ was a corn god but a corn god can accommodate an oak god.

Almost home. Up the lightly wooded, blacksoil Mount Debert track. Think of all the walkers have come through here. Up Taros Ladder, twenty climbing spikes driven into the cliff face about a metre apart, and I'm on the Narrow Neck plateau. It's time to swig some cool water and take a last look back.

I can see the waters of Lake Burragorang from Clear Hill. But that's not what I want to see now. I want to see that Carrington chimney, I want to see those Paragon chocolates.

On up the firetrail to Cliff Drive, an irritating sixteen kilometres. But what views! Just beyond Fool's Paradise the saddle is only fifty metres wide, you get a great view simultaneously of both Megalong Valley and Cedar Valley, behind Ruined Castle Ridge. And at the Narrow Neck gate I catch sight of the Three Sisters, across Jamison Valley. My journey is over and I feel glad I was born where so much remains to be done, not some place like Ireland, where you can walk in a few hours through what's left of the forests. Where the action is all in the past. But oak means more to me than eucalyptus, even blue gum, and that's a fact.

I must make love to the Fourth Sister without pursuing Her, without touching Her, without wanting Her.

She has eucalypts growing all over Her. Eucalypts are astounding trees. Botanists can't keep up with them, so rapidly are they evolving. They hybridise freely and are always being reclassified, shining their blue laser beams on the fault lines of Linnaean taxonomy. They are the shocktroops of a warming planet because they like firestorms, which civilized people don't. And the Blue Mountains is as good a place as any to make the acquaintance of these strange creatures, to get to feel their qualities, their variety. I never feel I possess them, or they me. I hardly dare divine their purposes. Their spirit, their genius, has yet to speak to me. I find them very dangerous.

Oh God it's great to be out of that park, to sip a coffee in Katoomba Street, to dig the ferals with their lip rings, to drift down to Echo Point and the Three Sisters, to see the floodlights again, to hear the polyglot voices, the charter coach auxiliary engines. I can't wait to get drunk. No more sweet black tea for the moment.

What I like about the Three Sisters, as seen from Echo Point, is the glade of green in Kedumba Valley beyond them, the promise of the crofter's life, a farm life surrounded by Wilderness. (I don't want to be a hunter-gatherer. Hunter-gatherers live in a world of sorcery.) This view must have hooked me as a kid, because I lead the crofter's life in the

Mountains now, as best I can, and though it lacks spiritual depth, I can't imagine there is a better physical life.

I survived. My quads feel good, my knee's ok. I've seen some birds and flowers that I hadn't seen before. And while the spirit of the eucalypt has not spoken to me, the spirit of the whistler and the pardalote has.

I've hit that Reset Button. I want to go on in the spirit of a bird in spring, I think the spotted pardalote. Hesitant. Persistent.

November 1996

Epilogue

Francis Barrallier left Australia in 1803, following a falling-out with Governor King over some social matter. Gregory Blaxland believed the four hundred hectares given him by Governor Macquarie as a reward for his journey were insufficient. He complained about this to anyone who would listen, and continued with his various schemes until committing suicide at the age of seventy-five. The more genial Henry Anthill retired from the army in 1825 and went to live near Picton. Elizabeth Hawkins' husband, Thomas, received a land grant of two thousand acres near Bathurst. She died in Surry Hills, Sydney, at the age of ninety-two. James Blackhouse and his companion, George Washington Walker, returned to England, but Walker came back to Hobart to live. Charles Darwin also returned to England, to write a best-selling account of his voyage around the world and to pursue his interest in the natural sciences. Louisa Meredith settled in Tasmania and wrote her *Some of My Bush Friends in Tasmania* and *Tasmanian Friends and Foes*. Sophia Stanger, whom the reader will recall as having shepherded five small children over the mountains, gave birth to four more babies after her arrival in Bathurst. She died in Bathurst in 1881, aged sixty-eight. At the time of going to press, the Wollemi pine seedlings were thriving at Mount Annan botanical gardens and David Foster, Australia's best living novelist, was about to take up employment as a deck hand on a fishing trawler in the Gulf of Carpentaria.

Sources & References

Extracts from the following sources for Chapters I to X have been edited fairly heavily to make them accessible to the general reader. Omissions are indicated by an ellipsis (...) except where they occur at the beginning or the end of an account. In some cases paragraphs have been broken up or run together, and footnotes have been included in the main body of the text. Spelling and minor aspects of style, such as the representation of numbers, have been modernised and standardised. I am grateful to Chris Cunningham's book, *The Blue Mountains Rediscovered*, for some of the information in the introduction and the notes.

General introduction and Chapter introductions: See bibliography

Chapter I: Barrallier, Francis, *Journal of the Expedition into the Interior of New South Wales 1802*, Melbourne 1975

Chapters II to X: These come from *Fourteen Journeys over the Blue Mountains of New South Wales 1813-1841*, edited and annotated by George Mackaness. This wonderful, scholarly book has been out of print for thirty years, and the present volume has the dual purpose of bringing about half of its material back into the public eye and of editing it to make it more accessible to the general reader. I have drawn on Mackaness's annotations for the introductions to each chapter, and for some notes within the extracts. The sources for Mackaness's collection are provided below. The chapter references refer to this book, not his.

II. Gregory Blaxland, whose journal was published in *Journal and Proceedings of the Royal Australian Historical Society*, vol. XXIII, part I, pp. 28-42. This has been heavily edited for the present volume, as Blaxland does not seem to have had much time for conjunctions or punctuation. The extract explaining his motivations comes from his letter of 28 November 1819 to John Bigge, the commissioner sent from London by the British government to inquire into Macquarie's rule.

III. Major Henry Anthill, from his journal, printed as No. 18 of the *Records of the Education Society* under the title 'Two Old Journals'

IV. Mrs. Elizabeth Hawkins, letter published in *Journal and Proceedings of the Royal Australian Historical Society*, vol. IX, part IV, pp. 177-197

V. Barron Field, *Geographical Memoirs on New South Wales*, London 1825. Thanks to Les Murray for the translation of the Italian phrase.

VI. X.Y.Z., *The Australian* newspaper, 13th March and succeeding issues

VII. James Blackhouse, *A Narrative of a Visit to the Australian Colonies*, London 1843

VIII. Charles Darwin, *Narrative of the surveying voyage of H.M.Ss. 'Adventure' and 'Beagle', Capt. [Admiral] P. Parker and [Admiral] Robert Fitzroy, 1826-36*, with *Journal of Researches into the Geology and Nautical History of the countries visited*, 4 vols., London 1839

IX. Mrs. Louisa Meredith, *Notes and Sketches of New South Wales during a Residence*, 1839-44, London 1844

X. Mrs. Sophia Stanger, *A Journey from Sydney over the Blue Mountains to Bathurst Forty Years Ago*, Bathurst 1882

Chapter XI :
Thanks to: Dave Noble, Wyn Jones, Bob Conroy (N.P.W.S.), Cathy Offord, Suzanne Bullock, Ken Hill (Royal Botanic Gardens, Sydney), Rod Peakall (A.N.U.), Jan Allen and the reports by James Woodford in the *Sydney Morning Herald*. Information on canyoning can be found at Dave Noble's home page *www.lisp.com.au/~daven*

Chapter XII:
Barrallier, Francis, *Journal of the Expedition into the Interior of New South Wales, 1802*, Melbourne 1975

Barrett, Jim, *Kowmung River*, Glenbrook 1993

Budawang Committee Press, *Fitzroy Falls and Beyond*, 1988

Macqueen, Andy, *Blue Mountains to Bridgetown. The Life and Journals of Barrallier*, Springwood 1993

Sloss, Robert, *Katoomba to Mittagong: Trekkers' Guide Book for the Ensign Barrallier Walk*, Mittagong 1991

Bibliography

Blainey, Geoffrey, *A Land Half Won*, Melbourne 1980

Blainey, Geoffrey, *Triumph of the Nomads*, Sydney 1978

Cunningham, Chris, *The Blue Mountains Rediscovered*, Sydney 1996

Foster, David, *The Pure Land*, Sydney 1974

Frost, Alan, *Botany Bay Mirages*, Melbourne 1994

Hardy, John & Frost, Alan (eds.), *Studies from Terra Australis to Australia*, Canberra 1989

Hughes, Robert, *The Fatal Shore*, London 1987

Mackaness, George (ed.), *Fourteen Journeys over the Blue Mountains of New South Wales 1813-1841*, Sydney 1965

Mosley, Geoff, *Blue Mountains for World Heritage*, Sydney 1989

Nicholas, F.W. & J.M., *Charles Darwin in Australia*, Cambridge 1989

Rolls, Eric, *A Million Wild Acres*, Melbourne 1984

Ward, Russel, *The Australian Legend*, 2nd edn, Melbourne 1965

Index of Places